SIX
SCOTTISH
BURGHS

SIX
SCOTTISH
BURGHS

CANONGATE PRESS

First published in Great Britain in 1992 by Canongate Press Plc,
14 Frederick Street, Edinburgh EH2 2HB

Text © Andy MacMillan 1992
Photographs © Ken MacGregor 1992

ISBN 0 86241 369 9

British Library Cataloguing-in-Publication Data
A catalogue record for this book is available on request from
the British Library.

Designed and keyed by Charles Anderson Design Consultants,
Quarriers Village, Bridge of Weir.

Printed and bound in Great Britain by Scotprint, Musselburgh.

Contents

For Angela and Lesley

The authors would like to thank the many people who willingly shared their specialist knowledge with us: the planners, librarians, curators and custodians, citizens and the worthies of the burgh - all proud of their towns and knowledgeable about them. I personally would like to thank Dr Bruno Del Priore and Kim Bellwood for their help in the beginning, and Canongate Press for their editorial support throughout.

Special thanks to my secretary, Catherine Stevenson, and her helper, Lesley Dwyer, for assistance well beyond any reasonable line. My thanks also to the film production team, both for their highly professional skills and their marvellously good natured tolerance of a tyro presenter, making the whole process both educational and enjoyable; and, above all, thanks to Ken MacGregor whose idea it all was.

Andy MacMillan
April 1992

What is a burgh ?

Many Scottish towns are proud to refer to themselves as burghs, seeing in that title a claim to a historic past, to a higher status once enjoyed, a title in retrospect now infinitely attractive in these days of bureaucratically imposed non-entity.Who would want to be a 'district', who had once been a proud city or burgh?

Not all Scottish towns were ever burghs, however; a burgh was a town with privileges accorded by a charter, usually, but not always granted by the king. Nor were all burghs royal burghs, which alone had the special privilege of self-government and the right to trade overseas and in imported goods. Later they acquired the right to attend parliament. Some burghs had been existing duns or forts, or even settlements but many were in effect 'new towns'.

In former times the burgh's privileges were significant: they included the right to enclose the town with walls and erect gates to close at night, or in times of danger; to elect a town council with bailies (magistrates); and to make their own by-laws. Perhaps the most important was that of forming merchants' guilds and trade incorporations with exclusive rights of manufacture and trade within the burgh and its 'liberties', a defined geographical area, usually coinciding with the sheriffdom of the castle.

There were also three rights of great economic value to the burghs: the right to hold markets, weekly or twice weekly, and fairs, annually or more frequently; the right to charge tolls; and the right of the merchants to claim exemption from the tolls throughout the kingdom. In return, the king would require loyalty from the burgesses and surrounding gentry and nobility, and help in the observation of his Royal Law, with responsibility for 'watch and ward' within the burgh, i.e. the keeping of the peace, incumbent on each burgess. Armed support in time of war was another obligation and burgesses were expected to provide their own arms and armour and to attend regular weapon practice or wappenschaws.

The burghs would give support to the royal exchequer through regular taxes in the form of a 'cess' on the burgh revenues from tolls and customs, supplemented by occasional contributions to specific events, such as a royal wedding or a particular military campaign. The burghs were thus a very important source of hard cash, of negotiable money, in an essentially barter economy.

To be a burgess was costly but profitable: it involved primarily the ownership of a toft or strip of burgh land within the walls, on which a house had to be built in a stated time and paying local taxes. Burgesses were elected and inheritance of a toft did not ensure the status of burgess for the heirs, unless they too were merchants in their own right at the time. Succession was a matter for the burgh court, as were the allocation of the duties of watch and ward. Later, a right of appeal from the burgh court was possible to a special Court of the Four Burghs (Edinburgh, Berwick, Roxburgh and Stirling). These, the earliest burghs, had uniform laws based on those of the English city of Newcastle upon Tyne. These common laws led to strong similarities in the physical form of the burghs.

The merchants' guild elected the town council and the provost, and, as their own spokesman, a Dean of Guild; sometimes both roles might be combined. The dean's normal remit was to adjudicate on matters of trading regulations and standards as well as on questions of property rights through his Dean of Guild Court. The various craft incorporations each appointed a deacon, who, in turn, elected as spokesman for the crafts, a deacon convener.

The town council, consisted of a regular number of councillors and bailies, often fixed by the charter, led by a praepositus or provost, originally the sheriff but later the chief magistrate, an elected position. These baillies had great power in the burgh court and were entrusted with the collection of taxes and adjudication of local disputes.

Just below them in the burgh hierarchy were a number of important officials: the town clerk, the official correspondent and keeper of the records; the chamberlain or keeper of accounts; the 'master of works'; the fiscal or public prosecutor who was also 'head of the watch' (or police). The list of sundry officials is too long to detail but could include lynsters who defined the boundaries, hangmen or executioners, the town crier, minstrels and pipers, inspectors, poinders and the 'supervisors of the common good' who looked after hospitals, almshouses and the like.

Most burghs had similar layouts and institutions. They were walled, with yett (gates), a Hie Gait (High Street), a hie kirk (parish church), a mercat or market place or places and a mercat cross, the visible symbol of their trading rights. A 'back walk' behind the walls was not uncommon. Each burgh would also have a tolbooth or town house (and gaol), a high school, and a protecting castle— most often that of the sheriff but occasionally a bishop would be the superior. Water-mills and wind-mills, tanneries, shambles or flesh markets, beast and grain markets, were functional attributes common to all early burghs.

A hierarchy of location usually followed from the siting of the kirk near the castle, with the nobles and important burgesses living in close proximity, and the flesh markets, tanners' yards and middens sited at the opposite end of the town, with the ordinary citizens distributed in between. The burghs, in effect, were rationally planned towns.

The earliest burghs date from the twelfth century, introduced by King David I, the ninth and youngest son of Malcolm Canmore and the third to ascend the throne. As a young prince, David had spent much of his youth at the court of his brother-in-law, Henry I of England. There he had experienced at first hand, the working of the feudal system which had been introduced some sixty years earlier by William the Conqueror. He came to appreciate its administrative merits, and as King of Scotland, brought the system back to his country along with experienced Norman knights of his acquaintance who, establishingcastles and fiefdoms throughout the lowlands, soon became almost more Scottish than the Scots themselves (the de Brus family, the Sinclairs, Maxwells, Frasers, Comyns, Beatons *et al*).

Using these newcomers, David created hereditary sheriffdoms to enforce the rule of Royal Law throughout his realm, but he also made a serious attempt to integrate the native earls and Celtic mormaors into his system, in an effort to unify his Kingdom. In the same spirit he invited the monastic orders of the Latin Church to settle in Scotland and provide care and learning, while encouraging farming and husbandry. Throughout the Middle Ages the monasteries were the repositories and the monks the proselytisers of science and learning.

Finally, David established burghs attached to castles or great churches or monasteries to stimulate industry and trade, especially overseas trade, and to provide example of the benefits of settled civilised life to the remoter parts of his realm. Dunfermline, Berwick, Roxburgh, Edinburgh, Stirling and Perth were among his earliest foundations.

For about 400 years the burghs proliferated and most flourished, reaching their heyday and present physical form in the sixteenth and seventeenth centuries. With the Union of the Crowns in 1707 the creation of new Scottish burghs ceased and other external forces directed urban growth throughout the United Kingdom. The burghs became part of a larger urban community, but even today retain a recognisable identity.

Arguably, they are the oldest towns in Scotland, even Edinburgh and Glasgow were respectively a royal burgh and a bishop's burgh. Today, when most of the population live in towns, some knowledge of what the burghs were is helpful to understanding the present urban environment. Most towns retain traces of their foundation and the influence of their original form persists even after centuries of change. Perhaps in looking at some selected burghs, a pattern of Scottish urban growth and change will become apparent.

The built fabric of a burgh is a tangible, physical record of its past and reveals the values of the present. The buildings have two stories to tell. First, the history of the burghs, as places of privilege, a set of towns with common characteristics which conditioned their development over a period of time, the story of why they were built. But there is another story, one concerned with the when and how they were built, the story of architecture. This tale touches on the materials and methods of construction, their use as centers and, most importantly, their civic intentions, their builders' views of their importance in and to the community. This architectural account unfolds broadly in five periods:

Medieval   from, say, around 1200-1400 AD the main period of castles, kirks and cathedrals, when the burghs were consciously conceived as a part of the elaborate social fabric of the feudal system, functioning as a counterpoint to the power of the landed nobility, and a source of revenue and loyalty to the Crown.

Renaissance   The sixteenth and seventeenth centuries in Scotland when the burghs achieved their most characteristic form. The buildings of the period largely have a pleasant vernacular character with occasional more elaborate public buildings or noblemen's palaces.

Georgian   The period immediately following the unification of Britain after the cessation of national warfare and the Union of the Crowns. A period of increasing urban density and consequently a more formal classical type of building characterises the eighteenth and early nineteenth centuries.

Victorian   The later nineteenth century can be seen as a period characterised by vigorous growth following the building of the railways and the burgeoning of industry. It is also, to some extent, the beginning of the destruction of the older fabric of the burghs.

Modern   Between and after the two world wars, a period of increasing expansion and suburban sprawl engendered by the invention of the petrol-driven vehicle, accompanied by massive destruction in historic town centres, culminating more recently in an awareness of 'heritage' and a review of attitudes to living in historic towns.

Each of these periods had its own characteristic urban and architectural forms, many of which continue to contribute to the rich mix that constitutes a contemporary burgh. Some burghs abound in the historic and present an attractive vernacular character; others are industrial or modern in appearance. In looking at a broad variety I hope that some understanding of the forces that variously shaped them can be gained, and something of folk history and the influence of invention and social progress discovered, as well as the familiar history of kings and battles.

I hope too you will enjoy some pleasure in looking at buildings and examining their forms and purposes, recognising similarities as well as differences, savouring the subtlety of details, clever or quirky, and in some cases even being excited by the splendours of the architecture. These are some of the possibilities underlying my choice of these six particular burghs: Stirling, a historic royal burgh, gateway to the Highlands; Paisley, a bustling tenement town in Scotland's central belt; Dumfries, a town in Scotland's south-west province and Kelso in the Scottish Borders— both flourishing market towns today despite a bloody past; Elgin, a remote yet urbane burgh; and Thurso, the most northerly town on the Scottish mainland.

Widely separated in space, differing in style but linked by their burghal origin, these towns have a diversity of robust character which should convey some idea of the richness of our Scottish urban inheritance.

I
ELGIN

Elegant, Classic, Classical

Elgin, the capital of the Laich of Moray, is named after Helgyn, the Norse general who founded it in the early years of the tenth century and it was one of the first Scots burghs created in the twelfth century, by that determined coloniser David I. His planned burgh and castle were sited on a protected bend in the River Lossie in the centre of the Laich, a great fertile plain on the north-east coast, isolated and protected to the south by the inaccessible mountains of the Mounth, and to the east and west, respectively, by those virtually unfordable rivers, Spey and Findhorn.

In 1224 Elgin became a city and the capital of the See of Moray when the Cathedral of the Holy Trinity was finally given a permanent site, thereby eliminating the influence of the old independent Scottish Church of the Culdees, in favour of the international Church of Rome, and bringing medieval Elgin into not only a national but a European orbit.

With the later establishment of Inverness as a burgh commanding the Great Glen, Elgin occupied a key position astride the principal road connecting the established lowland Kingdom to the more tenuously held Highlands of the west, ruled over variously by Norse Kings, Highland Lords of the Isles and Scotland's King himself. Macbeth reputedly slew Duncan here. He died of his wounds in the castle and Macbeth went on to rule ably for some seventeen years thereafter. David I was Duncan's grandson.

As was often the case Elgin had been a centre of habitation long before David's time, as surrounding prehistoric and pictish remains suggest, confirmed perhaps by the discovery in 1823 of a carved Runic stone in St Giles' graveyard in the very centre of the town confirms.

Duke of Gordon's Monument (1839)

The best place from which to view present-day Elgin is the castle motte at the west end, where under the Duke of Gordon's Monument (1839) can be found the ruins of the stone castle where Edward I resided twice, in 1296 and 1298. After his second visit the Scots themselves demolished it to dissuade him from ever coming back.

From this vantage point Elgin's original burgage structure can be perceived. Clearly falling into the classic high street pattern, it has a long main street stretching from thecastle at one end to the cathedral at the other, widening out in the middle to contain the mercat, mercat cross and high kirk. Another cross articulates the junction of the burgh and the Cathedral precinct. This was originally a separate walled entity known in medieval times as the canonry, composed largely of the dwellings of the ecclesiastics servicing the great cathedral church, which with its graveyard and gardens also stood within its walls.

From here, too, Elgin can be seen as classic in a different sense. Above the trees to the west is the splendid Georgian dome of Gray's Hospital, and to the east the fine lantern and portico of Anderson's Institution, while St Giles' neoclassic spire marks the town centre. All proudly proclaim the dignity of the Georgian rebuilding in the settled era following the suppression of the Jacobite Risings of 1715 and 1745.

The eighteenth and nineteenth century expansions and the twentieth century savagery or surgery of the traffic engineers is also visible.

Elgin's major urban asset is its virtually intact High Street, with its surviving narrow Burgage Rigs clearly visible both from above and at ground level. A stroll along the street from the Castle reveals the buildings from every important period of the burgh's history.

Descending from St Mary's Mound, as Castle Hill is now known, named for the medieval chapel, a relic of the castle, which once adorned it, you pass the First World War Memorial Gardens and baronial ex-servicemen's flats (1919) by J. & W. Wittet which stand beside a late 1970s housing scheme designed by the local Architects Department; the latter is beautifully landscaped, all fashionable monopitch roofs and harled detailing, attempting to create both a better impression and a sense of place. The original Blackfriars Monastery was sited behind the castle and the remnants of Murdoch's Wynd, after which the new housing is named, can still be seen just beyond the traffic roundabout.

The main part of the High Street is Victorian but a closer look and a walk up any of the pends, particularly on the north side, soon reveals the substantial remains of the seventeenth-century burgh.

In the first block there is a fine vintage 1930s chippie, the Northern Fish Shop, complete with formica tables and chrome trim, while across the road, the White Horse Inn proclaimed by painted sign, obviously occupies an original plot of some antiquity. A former landlady, Elizabeth Innes, was lauded by a local poet William Hay, in the following lines:

> Her name is Mrs Innes,
>   and the White Horse is her sign.
> O happy is the beast or man
>   that chances there to dine.

Across the way is the Victoria Bar, another collectors' bar which still has its *art deco* etched glass and original counter inside. Up a pend nearby, the Playhouse Cinema which originally had a front window on the High Street, was designed in 1932 by Alister MacDonald, son of Ramsey MacDonald, the Prime Minister, who came from nearby Lossiemouth and is buried in Old Spynie Graveyard.

On the left, at the entrance to the market is North Street, a wide street driven through the rigs in 1820, terminated by the Gothic entrance gable of the Episcopal Holy Trinity Church (1825), designed by William Robertson. Here is a case where the front elevation and the siting of the main door of a building were fixed by an urban axis rather than by any internal necessity.

Market Place and St Giles

The market place itself has a fine collection of public monuments. In the foreground, a Victorian three-tiered fountain (1844), now a multi-level planter, marks the site of the old tolbooth and stands in front of Percy Portsmouth's classic war memorial of 1920 making an interesting composition with the broad classical portico of Archibald Simpson's neoclassic St Giles (1825-8), built to replace the abandoned and ruinous gothic parish kirk.

Between the fountain and the portico are the Plain Stanes, a paved area built over the medieval graveyard in 1823 to form an 'exchange' or square between the old church and the tolbooth. Here in 1834 the last public hanging in Moray took place.

PARISH CHURCH OF ST GILES

Simpson, who transformed medieval and Jacobean Aberdeen into a new classical city of glistening granite in the early 1800s, was the architect chosen to build what is possibly the finest church of the Greek Revival in Scotland, proof of Georgian Elgin's determination to show a civilised example to the Laich of Moray. The subtlety of the church's proportions conceal its three-storey height, the broad sturdy Doric portico standing on the Plain Stanes seems to occupy the full width of the

market place. Unusually, St Giles' dominant tower, culminating in a replicated choragic monument to Lysicrates, stands at the rear of the church facing the other entrance to the market place. This creates a 'Janus'-like coming-and-going building with apparent fronts at each end. The scale is smaller to the east, more in keeping with the lesser market space.

This intriguing, beautifully proportioned church immediately establishes an unforgettable image of a cultured city, an impression consolidated by glimpses of Gray's Hospital whose dome dominates the route out to Inverness; and Anderson's Institution which terminates the town towards Aberdeen.

This trio of buildings must have been to Georgian Moray what the great medieval cathedral was to the region in the Dark Ages: a showy example of the benefits of an urbane society, a society which drew its strength from national and international connections, rather than parochial or kinship ties. Just beyond the church is the mercat cross (1670)—known locally as the muckle cross—removed in 1792 to assist traffic flow and reconstructed again in 1887, utilising the original carved Lion Rampant on a new shaft and steps. A cross has stood here since 1365, the present one modelled on the Renaissance version built in the reign of King Charles I.

But it is not all classical; the vigour of the Edwardian façades in this part of the town centre is unmistakable. Here the straightforward rules of classical architecture give way to personal invention and a stretching of the rules to accommodate the commercial building types of the era: the offices, warehouses and multi-storey department stores; which now line the street.

By contrast, a look up the pends below these impressive buildings reveals a wealth of historical details behind. Narrow wynds, burghal houses with datestones, marriage lintels, hanging lanterns, carved bulls' heads and so on; all well worth discovering.

A different kind of surprise on the north side is to find a top-lit modern shopping mall, entered through and behind the existing Victorian shops. No bad way of

Bull's head detail illustrates Edwardian individualism

inserting a new building type into a town of historic character; compare it with the disruption of the Norco Co-operative superstore and its car park at the eastern entrance to the High Street.

THE TOWER

Interesting historic buildings are to be found in the High Street. Opposite the muckle cross on the north side is the tower, the last remaining seventeenth-century laird's residence in the burgh. Built around 1634 by Alexander Leslie, an Elgin bailie, it is essentially a three-storey tower house, its circular stair with its crow-stepped square cap house above, projecting out into the street, and Leslie's armorial panel over the carved and moulded doorway. The main body of the building was exuberantly, if not cavalierly, 'improved' in 1876, and now presents an interesting confrontation of the real (the medieval original) and the idealised (the Victorian).

Issac Forsyth, an antiquarian and publisher, was a fascinating eighteenth-century tenant of the Tower. In 1789 (at the age of twenty-one) he founded the first circulating library in northern Scotland and also the Morayshire Farmers' Club as well as writing and publishing the Survey of the Province of Moray (1798).

At this end the market and the High Street are lined by fine seventeenth and eighteenth-century arcaded tenements, characteristic of a building type once widely prevalent in Scotland's towns and burghs. These three and four-storey tenements are pleasantly proportioned, usually with dormers and often articulated by crow-stepped gables, marriage lintels and date stones and have an arcade of carved columns and arches at ground level. The shops were originally set back behind the arcade to provide a Jacobean covered shopping mall.

The tenement at Nos 42-46 originally housed the Red Lion Hotel where Dr Johnson was served the only meal he had reason to complain of in Scotland. The central pend led presumably to the former inn yard. Nos 50-52, dated 1694 on the skew-put, was built by Andrew Ogilvy and Janet Hay; married women in those days often kept their own name as many tombstones and marriage lintels demonstrate.

Alexander Leslie's 17th-century tower with armorial panel

BRACO'S BANK

Near the Little or 'Mickle' Cross, Braco's Banking House is probably the best example, although like all the rest the actual arcade has been filled in; it was built in 1684, as the carved and monogrammed dormers tell us, for John Duncan and Margaret Innes.

The Duffs of Braco after whom it is named were a notorious banking family, who thrived on lending to estates following poor harvests and the failure of the Darien Scheme, and to forfeited Jacobite estates. Despite being so feared that even the Earl of Kintore was said to pray, 'Lord keep the Hill o' Foundlin between me and Braco', William of Braco prospered and, as his fortune grew, acquired property and joined the landed class. The family was able to commission James Gibbs to design the New House at Balvenie (1724) and, later, William Adam for Duff House (1735). By 1759, William, Lord Braco, had become Earl of Fife.

Braco's Banking House

Fashion and post-modern detail combine in Wm. Low's supermarket

THUNDERTON HOUSE

Back along the south side of the High Street, Thunderton Place, an older narrow wynd, leads to Thunderton House, now a bar and disco but once the King's House in Elgin, built in the sixteenth century as a Great Lodging to replace the castle. Later it became the town house respectively of the Earls of Moray, the Dunbars of Westfield and the Lords of Duffus. Once a huge courtyard palace with a great corbelled tower and its own gardens, it has fallen on harder times and is now much mutilated. The tower was removed in 1822 and with it went its grandeur. Enough remains, however, to give an impression of the past scale of the palace where Bonnie Prince Charlie slept in 1746 (where did he not sleep?).'Is it worthy of special preservation?' is a question which now might be asked for possibly the last time.

William Low's adjacent superstore is another exercise in the insertion of a large shopping facility into a small town (one wonders where all the customers for these stores are to come from? Will they all survive?). Some typical, pretty, post-modern details—fashionable cliches, if you like—enliven the walls in an effort to conceal the fact that the store is a great blank box, an attempt to minimise its bulk. It contains and conceals its own car park however, an admirable solution much to be preferred to the ubiquitous parking lots which disfigure so much of this town, and others. Across narrow Thunderton Place, the fashionable historical 'pastiche' approach to architecture can also be found in the form of a facsimile 'piazza' arcade. Is this right or relevant? Only the arch is used, not the set-back walkway. Similarly, a row of 1940s council houses out in Harrison Terrace to the north, utilises an isolated arch as an elevational device. Does all this devalue the originals? I suspect it does and think, too, that the genuine historical examples left should be properly restored and that the walkway behind the arches be reinstated.

Elgin's new facsimile 'piazza', complete with arches and lantern

A splendid little greengrocer's can be found in Thunderton Place, proudly displaying its Royal Warrant coat of arms as suppliers to the Queen Mother. It smells wonderful too, smell is a sense not always recognised or planned for nowadays, apart from, say, certain bread or coffee shops. Yet it can be a distinctive element of any city or town, e.g. the smell of brewing in Edinburgh or the sea at Anstruther, forms part of a distinctive sense of place.

Round the corner in South Street, the old Back Lane, can be found a number of exemplary period shops, a Victorian one with little columns, Murdoch & Clark; Bisset & Taylor's, a two-storey *art deco* shop-front alongside a splendid bull's head above the triumphal entrance arch (1851) of the former New Market.

On the other side of Fife Arms Close the splendid *art deco* lido cafe with its giant ice-cream cone outside, was built in 1927 as a soda fountain and *palais de danse* where the Lido Four played the latest jazz tunes. Alongside it is a long narrow picture house (1926), now the Caley Bingo, squashed into an old burgage plot with a simple front ruined by a clumsy roof. It is interesting nevertheless because it has only a front; the long side elevation is obviously not meant to be seen to exist - a very naive view of urban building but not uncommon.

Returning to the High Street, heading towards the cathedral, one finds that the completeness of the street begins to break down; newer 1960s housing and a shopping centre reduce the street scale and break the continuity of the urban wall with their horizontal emphasis even while attempting to pay tribute to the seventeenth-century arcades.

Across the street the Sheriff Court (1864) and a post-war municipal building also disrupt the street with their grassy setback. These buildings, which lie on the line of older individual houses which had individual private gardens with a railing on the street, are somewhat dull examples of both Victorian and recent architecture. Notice the old carved stones set in the arches of the gable facing the green, reminders of the town's history.

Opposite, one of the eighteenth-century tenements has a fine Palladian window on the first floor to signal the presence of a Masonic Lodge, attested also by Masoni Close behind. These tenements still have fine decorated dormers, a feature that soon ceased to be fashionable, replaced by powerful 'Renaissance Revival' cornices such as those of the Royal Bank of Scotland, 141-145 High Street, designed by Peddie & Kinnear in 1876.

Next door, what looks like a baronial drill hall, now an ex-services club, was actually the replacement in 1894 of an older laird's house. This is another case of pastiche being preferred to the original. The Victorians would certainly love Disneyland if they were around today. Beyond Braco's restored building is the 'Mickle' Cross with its steps, shaft and sundial. This cross was rebuilt in 1733, using possibly the carved finial of the original cross of 1402, erected as a penance by Alexander McDonald. Faced down by the Bishop and clergy of the cathedral while attempting his second spulzieing or despoiling in that year, he had it placed where it marks the boundary between the burgh and the chanonry.

Adjacent to the Mickle Cross, the Italianate Elgin Museum, 1 High Street, is a monument from those heady days when every burgh flourishing in the *pax Hanovarius* established fashionable, civilised institutions; the philosophical societies had their observatories and museums; the Assembly Rooms were for genteel social intercourse; and new hospitals, schools and kirks replaced the then run-down pre-Reformation originals. The Elgin Museum, designed in 1842 by Thomas Mackenzie, was founded by the Elgin & Morayshire Literary & Scientific Society, a body typical of this era.

The Mickle Cross, originally erected as a penance

Across the road behind the cross at 1 North College Street is a curious collage of a building with crow-stepped gables, a Renaissance upper half and Victorian lower half, redeemed by a pleasant, decorative, iron balustrade at the first-floor windows. Down the side of this building, the cathedral can be seen over the trees of Cooper Park, originally part of the chanonry, later the town house policies of the Earl of Seafield, and later still gifted to the town by Sir George Cooper.

The eighteenth-century Grant Lodge, now Elgin's Library (including a good local history collection), can still be discerned behind the coarse Victorian portico and bay window additions of the following century.

CATHEDRAL AND ITS PRECINCT

The Cathedral of the Holy Trinity is one of Elgin's glories and possibly the finest set of medieval church ruins in Scotland. That this great cathedral is to be found in the remote province of Moray in the far north of Scotland is a reminder of the power and the purpose of the church in the Middle Ages and its essential role in civilising and unifying Europe.

*Elgin
Cathedral*

Why else, if not to impress the barbaric fringe of his kingdom, would King Alexander the Second have encouraged Bishop Andrew of Moray to petition the Pope in far-off Rome to site this cathedral in his Royal Burgh of Elgin?

It can be likened to a sort of medieval West Berlin, a shining sparkling example of the 'good life', of the richness of opportunity that the Scottish kingdom might have to offer.

The repeated Highland burnings and spulzieings were perhaps an intuitive Gaelic understanding of the threat to their ancient culture that this building represented.

The Cathedral of the See of Moray had previously been variously sited at Birnie, Kinedder and Spynie (where the Bishop maintained his castle or palace), but in 1224 the then Bishop, Andrew of Moravia (or Moray), with the blessing of King Alexander II, successfully urged the Pope to allow him to permanently locate it in Elgin, by then well established as the centre of royal administration in the province.

Bishop Andrew also increased the Chapter of Canons from eight to eighteen, and then to twenty-three, making special arrangements to also constitute himself a member, thus emphasising the importance in the north of Elgin and the cathedral.

The first building was largely destroyed by accidental fire in 1270, and rebuilt thereafter somewhat larger in size and more splendidly in form. Virtually finished by the end of the thirteenth century, it was razed to the ground at the end of the fourteenth (1390) by Alexander Stewart, the second son of Robert II, the Earl of Buchan, better known as the Wolf of Badenoch, who had a score to settle with the bishop, and was spulzied again twelve years later by another Alexander, this time a son of the Lord of the Isles. Some traces of these burnings can still be seen in the existing fabric.

Tragic though the fires were they were nevertheless turned each time into an opportunity for a bigger and better re-building. As a result, the ruins today display many fine decorative features which give some idea of the cathedral's former glory.

The cathedral, with its supporting buildings and graveyard, sat within the chanonry, a walled mini—city adjacent to the burgh containing the residences of the various church dignitaries, canons and vicars in the cathedral's service. The best remaining example is the three-storey Precentor's Manse built in 1557. The south wing collapsed in 1891 but some idea of size remains. There were about twenty such manses in the chanonry.

Traces of the twelve foot high, three foot thick surrounding wall still remain, including Pann's Port, the old Water Yett and the last surviving medieval gateway, complete with portcullis slots but somewhat re-arranged by Victorian restorers.

The chanonry formerly included much of present-day Cooper Park, King Street, Cathedral Road and North and South College Roads. The wall surrounding Cooper Park was removed only in 1902, to be replaced by railings. The west façade, much of which remains today, is one of the cathedral's finest features, towering above the surrounding trees. Reminiscent of a French cathedral of the period, the lozenge between the doors would have held an image of the holy trinity in former times. The elaborate carved and moulded doorway, with its four-storey flanking towers, and ruined west window over, presented a wonderful triumphal arch and gateway between the profane world without, and the sacred world within.

From the South, the cathedral ruins still have character

Passing through it, the far end of the cathedral still stands giving some idea of its impressive length (270 feet) and a glimpse of its construction. The south aisle still retains its stone vaulted ceiling over which a timber and lead roof would have been erected. An impression remains, too, of the grandeur of the east end with its almost total curtain wall of tall lancet windows surmounted by a great rose window. Here in medieval times the ceremonial path to salvation would have ended at the altar in a blaze of glorious light.

Evidence of various rebuildings can be seen here. Notice, in particular, the deep clustered half-piers added beside the transept doorways, terminated not by an arch - as was clearly intended - but by huge decorative finials. Towards the end of the thirteenth century, this end of the church would have been most advanced in its design. Today we can only wonder at the daring of the masons and admire their skill in the multitude of carved and decorated features which still remain.

The octagonal Chapter House beyond the north aisle is a wonderful

Chapter House vaulting

demonstration of the masons' art, with its clustered central column and elaborate vaulted ceiling, where carved bosses mask the difficult joints at the meeting of the ribs and offer an opportunity for enrichment through decoration and coats of arms that tell of the cathedral's patrons and prelates. Look for the royal coat of arms on the central pillar and the amusing carvings in the windows, one of which shows a fox dressed as a friar preaching to a crowd of geese. Over on the back wall can be found the decorated seats of the Bishop, the Dean and Treasurer, the rest of the chapter having to be content with the simple stone bench that ran round the wall. Above their heads a number of memorial tombs adorn the walls, again telling us of the cathedral's important connections; many of these stones were placed there for safety in later years.

This Chapter House in which the dignitaries and canons sat to determine church policy has survived till today thanks largely to its post-Reformation role as the meeting place of the Incorporated Trades of Elgin, another body of worthy men who met with the interests of their calling at heart.

Between the Chapter House and St Columba's aisle can be found a little sacristy, where, legend has it, Elgin's great benefactor, General Andrew Anderson, was cradled in the lavabo by his mother who sought shelter in the ruins as a penniless soldier's widow who returned to Elgin after her husband had been killed in the war.

In the south aisle, the fine arched and encusped mural tomb of Bishop Winchester can be found, while in the remains of the south transept the visitor can see an effigy of a bishop and a knight from the former crossing tower and another pair of fine mural tombs, both now containing knightly figures.

Memorials and tombs also abound in the other transept and aisles while in the graveyard itself there are a number of aristocratic tombs and monuments such as those of the Earls of Murray, and the Dunbar and Innes families, and memorials of burgesses and members of the Incorporated Trades. Look out, particularly, for the various trade symbols and the skull and bones and winged heads, symbolic of death.

Three monuments in particular, deserve some mention. First the ninth-century Pictish cross-slab, placed in the cathedral graveyard in 1823 after its discovery under the old graveyard of St Giles, for the runic inscriptions on one side and hunting scenes on the other, a relic of pre-Roman church days.

Second, the monument to Elgin's own 'Old Mortality', the cobbler John Shanks, who, appointed to take care of the ruins in 1823 claimed, 'in the course of his life he had cleared away with his own hands, many thousand cubic yards of rubbish, collecting the carved figures and introducing some order and propriety' to the graveyard. His tomb can be found in the south east corner of the graveyard.

On the south-west boundary wall, a 1687 memorial displaying a glove and shears, is that of John Geddes, a glover. Carved on the face is this profound inscription rather reminiscent of the famous folk song of the sixties:

> this world is a city full of streets
> and Death is the mercat, that all men meets,
> if lyfe were a thing that monie could buy
> the poor could not live,
> and rich would not die

With the Reformation, the cathedral fell into disuse and disrepair, especially after the Regent Moray stripped the lead off the roof to help pay for his army. Some people perhaps thought that God had his own back when the vessel carrying the lead to Holland sank just off the shore.

By 1599 the buildings were so derelict that the Kirk Session saw the need to ban in the churchyard carol singing, guising, piping, violing and dancing. Women and lassies were also forbidden to haunt or resort to the kirk or kirkyard under the pain of public repentance. The end came when the crossing tower fell down into the nave in 1711. Thereafter the cathedral became merely a useful quarry for anyone building in the neighbourhood, a fate shared by many Scottish cathedrals.

No trace now remains of the early medieval alms-house of Maison Dieu, but one other medieval ruin of note can be found nearby. Greyfriars' Monastery, which originally lay at the east end of the High Street just beyond the burgh. It had been gifted in 1479 by John Innes of Innes to the Oservant Branch of the Franciscan Order, only to be sacked in 1560. In 1895 the 3rd Marquess of Bute hired John Kinross to restore its ruined fifteenth-century church and renovate the conventual buildings as a private Catholic school.

Bute was a noted medievalist having previously restored both Cardiff Castle and Castle Koch in Wales, and built Mount Stuart, his huge neo-gothic house in Bute.

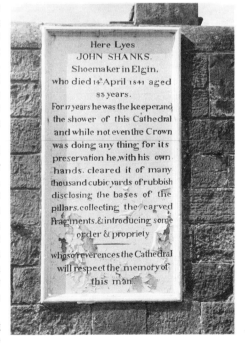

John Shanks' gravestone at Elgin Cathedral

22

GEORGIAN ELGIN

This is an example of how private benefaction has assisted, maintained and strengthened the identity of our burghs over the years. A sentiment which nicely brings us to Georgian Elgin.

A fascinating aspect of burgh life is the continuity of its cultural institutions kirk, hospital, school. Formerly functions of the Holy Mother Church and its religious orders, after the Reformation it increasingly fell to the burghs to ensure their provision, often from the revenues of former church lands, but also not infrequently by private benefaction. Elgin was well served in this latter aspect, particularly by its two great nabobs, men who earned great wealth in the service of the Honourable East India Company before returning home to their native city.

One was Dr Alexander Gray, who founded the hospital bearing his name and also made a handsome contribution to the new church. The other was General George Alexander Anderson, who endowed the Elgin Institution for the support of old age and education of youth. The trustees of both these philanthropists employed the best architects of the day, for the hospital: James Gillespie Graham, the fashionable Edinburgh architect, and for the Institution, an equally fashionable architect from Aberdeen, Archibald Simpson, who was already engaged in the rebuilding of the church.

James Gillespie Graham, architect of the Hospital

Gray's Hospital

GRAY'S HOSPITAL

Dr Gray's Hospital lies at the west end of the town. Twenty thousand pounds was left for its provision by Dr Alexander Gray, who died in 1816. Built between 1815 and 1819, it is one of the finest neo-classical buildings in Scotland. Interestingly, its foundation stone was laid on the same day in 1815 as news of the Battle of Waterloo reached Elgin.

A splendid, beautifully proportioned dome bestrides the skyline above a simple three-storey block ennobled by

full-height pilasters and a projecting central Tuscan portico. The upper row of attic windows at some time has been enlarged and perforates the entablature and cornice; daylight versus beauty, one supposes, perhaps a sign of the times, the servants no longer willing to suffer that others might enjoy the building.

Notice the elegant way the dome and cupola sit first on a round masonry drum, translated then to an octagonal, and finally, a square base on the portico. This is a subtle building which will repay scrutiny with pleasure. It has recently been completely refurbished as a modern hospital.

The Elgin Institution

Simpson's H-shaped Elgin (or Anderson's) Institution, built between 1830 and 1833, has a stunning front elevation, with pedimented wings and a fine Ionic portico surmounted by the founder's statue, appropriately supported by an old man and a young girl. Round the corner, a simpler Doric portico faces the garden, while behind lies the Free School. A fine domed lantern surmounts the whole to provide a marvellous termination to the east end of the High Street, matching the magnificence of the hospital to the west.

The institution originally housed ten elderly men and women and fifty children (it continues today to house the indigent elderly), while its industrial school provided for the care and education of children of the labouring classes whose parents could not support them, and for their placement in useful industry thereafter. A Free School was also incorporated which provided for the education of a total of 230 children.

Simpson's St Giles, the hospital and the institution (the Industrial School was part of the institution as was the Free School), form a trio of unforgettable urban monuments, a fine tribute to the peaceful era which followed the final defeat and integration of the Highland kingdom.

This Georgian era was a busy one in Elgin and many other lesser buildings were renewed or replaced in these times of peace.

VICTORIAN ELGIN

With the coming of Victoria's reign, new types of buildings proliferated: banks, schools, assembly rooms, masonic halls, inns, livery stables, hotels and a flourish of churches not to mention the lavish provision of new and salubrious homes for the rapidly expanding entrepreneurial classes.

This was when the building of Elgin's 'new towns' or suburbs took place. Characterised by expansion to the south and a doubling of the size of the burgh, the coming of the railway saw New Elgin established as a working-class or artisan suburb while another middle-class suburb grew up to the north at Bishopsmill. New Elgin, consisting essentially of simple cottages, has a park to the west where you can find a children's playground, a striking mural in the park shelter, and a fine beehive-shaped doocot, somewhat sadly neglected. 'Doos' or pidgeons were a source of winter meat for the laird and a source of contention with the farmers whose crops they consumed.

The first expansion of the burgh's core centred on School Wynd, later renamed Commerce Street, in anticipation of the trade it was hoped the railways would bring. The Georgian development began in South Street, which was initially taken over by inns and stables, but with the prospect of settled times the need to build and to extend the town grew pressing and a new suburb of villas was developed along the axes of Moray Street and Moss Street. Reidhaven Street is characterised by pleasant but unpretentious small Georgian houses, while Moray Street, which ran parallel to the High Street, tended to attract the first flush of institutions, such as the Unitarian Free South Church of 1853, a simple early Victorian gothic church.

Further along Moray Street is Elgin's second academy, designed by the Reids in 1885. It replaced an earlier Georgian building of 1801 in Academy Street and combined the old academy and the music school.

Elgin's original academy had been founded in 1566 just six years after the Reformation taking over from the church schools; the burgh employing the former ecclesiastics as teachers, and in 1594 James VI & I had made over the old Maison Dieu lands to the town to provide for a new alms-house and also provide teaching in music. The Academy recently moved out to the north in the 1960s and a new College of Further Education was built in the grounds.

Victoria School of Science and Art

Facing the Academy, diagonally across the street is the Victoria School of Science & Art (1894), erected to commemorate Queen Victoria's diamond jubilee. This school, which had its origins in the old Elgin Drawing School, looks more like a church than an academy, and has some interesting carvings and cast-iron rainwater pipes with dragons, and is much more interesting than the mundane Academy or uninteresting Free South Church alongside.

The Town Hall (1885), gigantic and turreted formerly stood in Moray Street too, adjacent to the Academy,

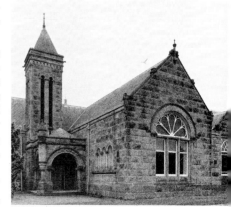

enhancing its importance, but in 1939 it was burnt out and a dull replacement built later on the High Street.

Queen Street has some fine houses, particularly the Greyfriars House of 1846 which is extravagantly detailed and pleasantly composed about its entrance. At the top of this street is another little growth of elegant Victorian houses, and just round the corner, the lodge to the old Elgin Free School has an eye-catching Dutch gable and twisted chimney. At the foot of Duff Avenue - a street of fine, large-scale villas - lies the Lodge (1898), a curiously personal composition of pediment and corner towers. The Reids, who were local, were certainly the kind of Victorian rogue architects who could freely manipulate rules and elements.

House by G.R.M. Kennedy

Next door, in part of its garden, is a fine contemporary house by G.R.M. Kennedy, designed for and built by a builder with whom he worked. The steeply angled monopitch roofs are handled with assurance and the building is very well built, an interesting contemporary addition to Elgin's villa stock.

Another modern treat can be found in the west end of the town beyond the hospital. An unexpected surprise in Wittet Drive, a street of pleasant little bungalows, is to come across at No 13 a single-storey, 1930s-style gleaming white gem (though completed after 1945), whose architect-developers J. & W. Wittet had intended that all the bungalows would look like it.

However, public opinion then as now was far too conservative, even without the help of Prince Charles.

This flat-roofed little house is absolutely typical of its genre and has recently been carefully restored by its new owners who even approached the original manufacturers for replica windows. Something of a local celebrity now, it has been listed for preservation by a sympathetic local council.

Bungalow on Wittet Drive, 1930s-style

Turning right at the top end of the drive, an unusual group of late Edwardian

houses can be found on the opposite side of West Road, the old turnpike to Inverness. The enjoyable thing about the Edwardians was their sheer exuberance and lack of restraint. This set of small houses is a fine example of their uninhibited approach to architecture. No Georgian decorum here, instead a terrace of houses boldly designed to look like a city wall, incorporating old salvaged stones taken from demolished historic buildings. Look closely at the semi-detached disguised as a castle with its battlements and stained glass windows; and the astonishing bungalow, No 19, a witch's house from Fairyland with colossal stones and fantastic dome and twin bay windows. They say the builder, who built this one for himself, had visited America. Was it Texas one wonders? At the rear, is an exiting belvedere and a splendid spiral stair down a small cliff. A wonderful Renaissance satyr's face carved on what looks like a pulpit, possibly taken from nearby Spynie Palace, can be f o u n d alongside the stair. This is p r i v a t e property but the owner may well

Carved satyr from Renaissance period

The Edwardians' unique style: 'luff battlements' and bewitching pillars and dome

allow you to view it if you ask permission, or if you choose to board there.

These houses, the remarkable achievement of a local builder probably with the help of a local architect with whom he collaborated, are a treasure worth seeking out, the kind of eccentric personal gesture that may be 'not quite architecture' but is splendid fun, and makes for a strong sense of place.

THE MILLS

The New Mill Museum

Behind these houses Old Mills Road runs down to the riverside and on over the Bow Bridge (1630-5), Elgin's first stone bridge, passing on the way, Old Mills, one of the finest working mill museums in the country. This is a generic, functional building type found in all burghs, an early industrial building, fascinating also for the sophistication of its machinery made of iron, wood, leather and rope, not to mention the actual grindstones themselves. Such mills represented a huge capital investment and often constituted an enforced monopoly service whose returns went to kings, sheriffs, bishops and burghs.

Tanneries were another building type found in all burghs, but few now remain. Their frequent mention however is a reminder of the importance of leather as an industrial and commercial material in former times, not merely for shoes and handbags, or the odd piece of clothing, but as the only naturally waterproof material. On account of its toughness and elasticity, its use for industrial purposes was widespread: saddlery, reins, carriage springs, driving belts for machinery, gaskets on boats where masts passed through the hull etc. and a thousand and one other uses, now served by newer synthetic or metallic substances. Unfortunately few tanneries are to be found now.

The King's Mill, the first mill on the Old Mill's site, was clearly in use well before Alexander II granted it and its rights to the monks of nearby Pluscarden Abbey in 1230. The present mill building, now called Old Mills, dates from approximately 1793, the kiln and storage area being added in 1850. Now as a Mill Museum with a Ladeside Nature Trail attached, this simple stone and slate building is a fine example of 'unconscious' vernacular architecture, predicated only by function and building technology.

The mill has two wheels, one on each side, and the weir divides the river into three streams, one for each wheel and one to carry excess water away; both wheels are 'Breast Shot' or drop the water mid way up the wheel and drive a toothed pit wheel internally, which in turn drives the grinding machinery. The teeth are timber to avoid sparks as fine flour dust is always present in any mill.

Modern Elgin Academy can be seen across the River Lossie from the mill, a fine example of the flat-roofed functionalist buildings of the 1960s looking well in the rural landscape.

As well as the Old Mills the burgh formerly had a Bishop's Mill and a Sheriff's Mill, their caulds or cruises still visible by the banks of the Lossie. Newmill and Lossiebank Mill (1797), upriver at Deanshaugh, are larger-scale industrial mills built for the manufacture of tweed, both good examples of industrial vernacular architecture. Simple in form, decorated with a cupola and well-shaped windows, by 1868 Newmill was the largest employer in the town. Some parts of the complex remain, including a mill shop.

Over the nearby iron Sheriffmills Bridge (1803) lies the free-standing villa of Connet Hill, built in 1913 by A. Marshall Mackenzie with a flavour of Regency, but clearly a forerunner of modern architecture to come and one which helps set its evolution in its historical context. This villa is seen to particular advantage from West Road.

Another episode in the history of modern architecture can be found at the west end of Murray Drive, in Hay Street. There stands a fine 1930s block of flats by J. & W. Wittet. Sadly, the craze for double glazing has removed many of the original horizontal window bars giving a somewhat blank stare to the building; it would be appropriate if these horizontal mullions could be reinstated. The post office is undistinguished, and the 1960s Town Hall, by Kininmonth & Spence, sited conveniently to the bypass and for easy parking, faces rather unfortunately away from the town; a pity because clearly the Elgin tradition of going to good architects had been continued in this instance.

The stained-glass mural in the rather anachronistic 1950s headquarters building for Scottish Malt Distillers across the road is worth a visit. From here, too, the half-finished (at the time of writing) glass pyramids of the new superstore behind the High Street look interesting and somehow in keeping with the roofscape of the backlands.

What is extraordinary about Elgin is its sheer urbanity, the strength of its High Street in maintaining its sense of place, and the outstanding, absolute quality of its monuments: Anderson's Institution, St Giles Church, and Gray's Hospital and, of course, the cathedral. Elgin also very clearly demonstrates the persistence of the site pattern of the original burgh, and constantly reveals the intentions of its founding burgesses and their descendants to show a civilised example to the surrounding area.

The wise choice of good architects in the past has left it a wonderful legacy to hand on, and the worst excesses of the twentieth century seem to have been just avoided. Can it be hoped that rather than resting on their laurels—having preserved what is good from their past—the present burgesses will find that same courage to provide their heirs with buildings of today of equal quality, and not be fobbed off with what is convenient, economic or even simply adequate.

II

DUMFRIES

Bruce and Burns; Peter Pan, the Bluebird and the Royal Welly Boots.

Situated a few miles inland from the Solway Firth at the upper tidal reach and lowest bridging point on the River Nith, Dumfries was the first burgh in south-west Scotland. William the Lion (1165-1214) built a castle here in 1179 and, seven years later, created a royal burgh to support it, thus continuing the Anglo-Norman policy of his father, King David I, of subjugating and controlling the kingdom through castle, church and burgh. William conferred his new burgh on Jocelin, Bishop of Glasgow, at about the same time as gifting its church and some adjacent land to St Peter's Hospital in York, an indication of the uncertain concept of nation in those days, when a baron or even the King of Scotland might also hold land in England, for which he would owe allegiance there.

The name Dumfries, pronounced 'Drumfreesh' locally, is Gaelic in origin, either from Dronfres 'the ridge of the bushes', or Dumfries 'the fort of the corpse', and the area abounds in Neolithic and Bronze Age remains, indicating a settlement of considerable antiquity. Protected by the great Lochar Moss to the east, the River

Nith to the north and west and small river later called the Milburn to the south, it occupied an important strategic position commanding the river crossing of the pilgrims' route to Whithorn Abbey and Galloway and, beyond, to Ireland.

In those medieval times not only were Galloway and Dumfriesshire virtually a separate kingdom inhabited by native Picts and Celts from Ireland, but the south-west itself was an area of great contention between self-willed warring barons as well as between the kingdoms of Scotland and England, and changed hands regularly and bloodily. During the Wars of Independence Dumfries was burned by the English on at least seven occasions, and burned itself accidentally on another four (the usual Scots own goal). Thus, though few residential or religious buildings of that era have survived, castles abound, some in good repair, others ruined.

BRIDGE

The best place to begin to look at historical Dumfries is probably from the old medieval bridge. Still called Devorgilla's Bridge, the present stone structure was

built in 1431 by the then Earl Douglas to replace an earlier wooden bridge which had been swept away in a flood. It had been gifted to the burgh in the thirteenth century by Lady Devorgilla Bailiol, daughter of Allan, the last Celtic King of Galloway, and niece of King David I of Scotland. She was one of the two great ladies associated with Medieval Dumfries; the other, Princess Margaret, was the daughter of Robert III and wife to Archibald the Grim, 3rd Earl of Douglas.

Devorgilla and her husband John Baliol the Elder were the founders of Balliol College in Oxford and five years after his death in 1269 she founded St Mary's Abbey near Dumfries, in his memory. This was the last

Devorgilla's Bridge

Cistercian Abbey to be established in Scotland. The word 'sweetheart' has come into the language as a popular term of endearment because after Baliol's untimely death she had his heart embalmed and sealed in a lead and ivory casket which she then kept by her as a constant reminder of his presence. Some twenty-one years later (c.1290) she had herself interred in the Abbey, clutching her 'sweet heart' to her bosom. Her much-mutilated effigy is to be seen on top of a reconstructed tomb in the south transept of the Abbey.

Devorgilla was also responsible for an invitation to the Franciscans to found a Minorite Friary in Dumfries, granting them the tolls from the bridges for their support. It was in their Greyfriars' Church that Bruce stabbed Sir John Comyn, the 'Red Comyn', to precipitate the War of Independence which made Scotland a free nation, with Bruce himself its king.

Unfortunately no trace now remains of either the friary where the famous European Medieval scholar, John Duns Scotus, took the vows and habit of St Francis, or of the royal castle, captured in turn by both Wallace and Bruce, other than a rectangular motte and commemorative stone in the Castledykes Park. The stone castle was demolished by the Scots to prevent its occupation by the English armies.

SWEETHEART ABBEY

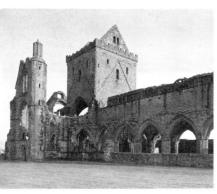

Sweetheart Abbey, however, is still standing, though now a splendid ruin. Its great granite boundary wall is the finestremaining Medieval demesne wall in Scotland and the huge red sandstone church towers over the pleasant little vernacular village, New Abbey, which clearly grew up out of, and about, the abbey after the Reformation. The village has some fine set pieces to be enjoyed in the behind a topiary hedge, an attractive Masonic Lodge and an Odd Fellows Hall, a picturesque Victorian porch with barley-sugar columns and a vernacular cottage with carvings, probably salvaged from the ruined Abbey.

Sweetheart Abbey -still magnificent

A particularly fine Georgian working corn mill now occupies the site of the Medieval Monks' Mill, its mill pond and monastic fish pool, still there to be seen within the abbey demesne. They serve as a reminder of the function of the monasteries and abbeys of the Middle Ages as repositories of the scientific knowledge and skills of the Roman Empire through the Dark Ages. An important role, less well appreciated than their better-known functions as the religious, administrative, educational and health centres of the Medieval era, but related to the close association of monastic establishments with systematic farming, proper husbandry and the management of gifted lands; with schooling, reading, writing and recording, and with law, all aspects of scholarship. The monastic library was an archive of knowledge of all sorts, not just of religious texts. The provision of medical care in the Medieval community was a major service and

Working Georgian corn-mill, on the site of the Medieval Monk's Mill

the herbarium was an adjunct of the infirmary.

These various functions were all integral parts of a multinational religious organisation spread across Europe with its headquarters in Rome.

In the feudal system, the church and its religious orders had a serious part to play in the organisation and unification of the kingdom, something clearly understood by the Norman incomers and the successive normanised kings of Scotland who, in their own interest, effectively rooted out the old independent Scottish Culdee Church in favour of the interactive Roman Church. David I introduced the system of a priest in every parish as a counterweight to the secular authority of the barons

Enough remains of Sweetheart Abbey to see its general form, the huge church oriented east and west, faced in red sandstone on a core of granite river boulders, with its conventual cloister and out-buildings adjacent. The great gabled tower dominated the surrounding landscape, its bell punctuated and controlled the working day with regular calls to prayer. Inside the church a stone slab marks the site of the former high altar, while over in the south transept (crossing), the tomb of Devorgilla can be found.

The Abbey's huge bell tower

Around the cloister can be seen the remains of the Sacristy where the priests robed, the Chapter House where they deliberated, and the Warming House, the only place where a fire was provided. All these still exist above ground with some interesting decorative detail and foundations at ground level, outlining the position of the kitchen, dining room, day rooms and dormitories. The lay brothers, that is those abbey workers who were members of the community but not members of the religious order, were housed in a range of buildings alongside the road nearer the public entrance to the abbey, where the visitors' hospice would also be sited.

A fair amount of decorative work and moulding remains despite the ravages of the Reformation and the subsequent quarrying of the abbey for building stone. The arrangement of the west window is curiously asymmetrical and the south transept has an interesting wheel window oddly interrupted by the adjoining roof.

NEW ABBEY MILL

No visit to New Abbey should omit a tour of the early eighteenth-century mill, whose workings interestingly reveal the miller's role in Medieval society, essentially as that of an engineer, concerned as much to oil and lubricate the machinery and keep it in good working order, as well as his specialist role in the roasting and grinding of the corn. This mill has an unusual but highly effective pitchback wheel which turns against the flow of water. The simple functional buildings of the mill are elegantly proportioned, shaped by function and animated by purpose. They are a useful prototype against which to judge similar functional buildings of the eighteenth and nineteenth centuries to be discovered in Dumfries.

LINCLUDEN COLLEGE

Another important Medieval remain can be found in Dumfries: Lincluden Collegiate Church where Princess Margaret of Scotland is entombed. Originally a small convent of nuns, it was taken over, endowed and expanded by Archibald the Grim, 3rd Earl of Douglas, when David II granted him the Lordship of Galloway. He banished the nuns and substituted a college of priests to pray for him and his family in perpetuity, possibly the sign of a guilty conscience

The college is sited in a bend of the River Nith where the Lincluden Burn joins it and contains an early motte, the ruins of the college and its church, and an interesting grassed over geometric mound, the remains of a Renaissance formal garden. The site is said to have been a favourite visiting spot for Burns and his son. Did his son play on the motte and the mound, out of the way, while father contemplated of the romantic ruins and composed?

The church, endowed by Archibald's son, the 4th Earl, is reputedly the work of John Morrow, a Parisian-born master mason who worked at Melrose Abbey. This Archibald was also Duke of Touraine and presumably *au fait* with current French fashions in architecture. The tomb of his wife, Princess Margaret, daughter of Robert III, has pride of place in the left-hand side of the church, within a sumptuously carved and crocketed recess. Her effigy lies on an arcaded bench, above a row of heraldic shields proclaiming her royal pedigree. The adjacent doorway to the porch is equally elaborate and the adjoining block, the Provost's Lodging, has a vaulted ground floor and an octagonal turnpike stair with gun ports. This block is of a later date – early sixteenth-century – and was still in use as a residence well into the second half of the seventeenth century.

Ad hoc but not unattractive additions to the chapel decoration, are the fine carved graffiti displayed in the nave in upright Roman as well as a fine cursive script. The act of decoration can be seen to derive from a human instinct to leave a mark on an empty space, to personalise or make particular undifferentiated space. Directed, this urge becomes creative, becomes decoration which by its nature and its use makes the place or the building legible, for example the crocketed niche containing the effigy, by its accentuation, announces clearly the importance or social significance of the figure within.

At this point, if we leave the college and make our way back to the centre of town we can gain a good impression of the form of the burgh from the rebuilt bridge of Archibald, the 3rd Earl. The oldest house in Dumfries is not in the burgh itself but across the river at the Maxwelton end of the bridge; Bridge End House, built in 1662 is now so altered as to be virtually undatable. One of the local museums, it contains a number of historic artefacts, and has some reconstructed apartments from various periods in the town's recent history, including a dentist's surgery.

Clearly visible from the bridge on the Dumfries side are not only an infill of seventeenth and eighteenth-century building on Whitesands, the riverside horse and cattle market, mostly bars, inns and contemporary fast-food outlets, but immediately behind on the high ground, a row of fine Georgian mansions along Irish Street. Sadly the building up of the riverside retaining wall has obscured the position of the old ford at the foot of Nith Place (clearly visible in older photographs) but the Nith is a river still liable to major flooding, as a look at the steps on the new waterside Royal Bank of Scotland shows. This is a rather pleasant building by Rowand Anderson & Partners, modern but sympathetically built in the local Locharbiggs red sandstone but clearly contemporary in its lavish use of glass.

20th-century construction as used by the Royal Bank

TOWN MILL

The last remaining eighteenth-century town mill across the Nith from the Royal Bank of Scotland is now a Burns Heritage Centre. Originally it was an important municipal mill, necessitating the building of the caul, or weir which directs the river towards the mill lade. This fine piece of eighteenth-century industrial engineering has had to be repaired on at least four occasions after damage by floating ice in the winter thaws. The mill is fairly direct and simple, again built in the ubiquitous red sandstone and sits in a pleasant park with an adjacent deer park and children's playground.

ORIGINAL BURGH

On the ground, and on contemporary maps, the area of the original burgh can still be seen despite the well-intentioned but disastrous ravages of those so-called improvers: the twentieth-century developer and the planner.

Castle Street commemorates the castle which formerly stood at the head of the burgh to the north. Below it to the south along the ridge was the High Street widening out into a broad market space defined by Queensberry Street to the east and High Street to the west. Narrow tofts ran off each side to Loreburn Street, originally the line of Loreburn which ran alongside the Lothar Marsh and Irish Street, the old east and west Barnraws respectively. In the later Medieval era the broad market space was largely built over, to the north by the New Wark, a large Medieval residence and stronghold, built by Lord Maxwell, to replace the castle as a presence in the town and towards the south, by a tolbooth and gaol, and some dwelling houses (where Burtons now stands). English Street surely self explanatory, was originally the Lochmaben Gait and Shakespeare Street, both of which generated another set of tofts at right angles to those of the High Street. Nith Place led down to Whitesands, and to the ford.

The Minorite Friary and, later, some further tofts were developed westwards along Friars' Vennel towards Devorgilla's Bridge. Lastly, to the south, St Michael's Church and churchyard developed beyond the South Port as the principal church of the burgh. Other Medieval gates, or yetts, were sited on the bridge, on Townhead Road (now Edinburgh Road), at the junction of Lochmaben Gait and Shakespeare Street.

Buccleuch Street and the New Bridge were late additions in the eighteenth century, the first major expansion beyond the burgh in the wake of agricultural improvement and the American tobacco trade subsequent to the Act of Union. Much later a third bridge, the Suspension Bridge, was built for the convenience of mill workers crossing the Nith, and in 1972 St Michael's Bridge was added to cope with growing traffic and assist it bypass the town centre.

PORTS

Whitesands was not only the beast market but also the original town port for shallow-draught river and coastal craft, Dumfries having a considerable shipping trade, with imports predominating over exports. After the Act of Union, trade developed with America with tobacco and cotton imported and hides, grain, cattle, sheep and pigs as exports. A quay wall was built in the mid-eighteenth century and extended to form the dock now transformed into Dock Park, where an interesting monument commemorates two local sailors who died in the sinking of the *Titanic*. Later still, a new dock and warehouses were constructed at nearby Kingsholm and a new port at Glencaple further down the river.

Many of these earlier developments were the outcome of the improved communication system of turnpike roads, made possible by the pacification of the country after the Jacobite Risings, when carts from the ports would make their way to Dumfries and destinations beyond. Until the coming of the railways in 1848 the Wednesday loading of the long-distance carriers' carts in Queensberry Place was one of the sights of the town, similar, perhaps, to the setting-off of the wagon trains to the American West. These carriers provided a link with the rest of the country and beyond, often being two or three days away on their journeyings. Hence the proliferation of inns and hotels to serve the developing markets, the carriers and the new 'county' travelling public. The regular stagecoach services made such accommodation both necessary and possible. The King's Arms, the County Hotel, the Queensberry and the George, all served the stagecoach trade. The commercial and the railway hotels followed after for the railway trade; the later second Railway Hotel (1896) is rather a fine Edwardian red brick and white wood building with a delicate cupola and interesting dormers.

The former King's Arms Hotel, now merely a rebuilt façade, was not only the local Whig headquarters and the scene of Burns's official Excise Dinners but, in February 1829, it was the scene of the largest riot in Dumfries, when a crowd of thousands attempted to lynch Hare, who, with Burke, had been notorious as the Edinburgh body-snatchers. Burke had been tried and executed, but Hare, having turned king's evidence, had been granted a free passage to Ireland via Port-Patrick. When he and his companions attempted to spend the night in Dumfries, the news spread quickly and an angry mob rioted. Only prompt police action and the use of a decoy allowed him to escape via England, and when his sister called six months later to collect his clothes left behind in haste, she was shown them still lying in a corner—no-one would touch them.

Modern inhabitants of Charles Edward Stuart's old room

Sadly, and astonishingly, the room in which Bonnie Prince Charlie conducted his business during his occupation of Dumfries in 1745 was preserved well into the 1980s when the old County Hotel was gutted and the room demolished to make way for a new branch of Next. Could this really happen in a civilised country in Europe? What is the point of a vaunted planning system if vandalism like this is possible?

INNS

The market and the carriers were served by a variety of inns such as the Globe (Burns's favourite howf), the Coach & Horses (haunt of Maggie Hogg, a local prostitute immortalised by Burns as Muirland Meg), the Three Crowns, and the Hole in the Wall (dating from 1620) in the High Street and the Ship Inn in St Michael's Street. Today the Whitesands and Friars Vennel areas still have a concentration of bars and their modern descendants, the fast food-chains, many more noisy than necessary.

WHITESANDS

Whitesands was not only the site of the weekly cattle market and the twice-yearly horse fair, but frequently, too, the scene of public execution. Here Covenanters were shot after the ill-fated rising of 1666, when the local anti-bishop forces captured the King's Military Governor and carried him off to Edinburgh, only to be routed and scattered by Dalyell's Royalist cavalry on the way. Some 160 of the survivors were put to death or transported. The heads and right arms of the Covenanters shot on Whitesands were cut off and exhibited on the arches of the Toll Bridge for all to see. A plaque commemorates the execution of James Kirk, shot on the sands in 1685

Here too during the 'witch'-hunts of the late seventeenth century unfortunate women and men were tortured and then burned on Whitesands as a public spectacle. The executioners, who strangled the victims before igniting the pyre, were frequently paid in ale. Dumfries was the scene of the last judicial trial for witchcraft in Scotland in 1709 when a woman called Elsbeth Rule was found guilty, branded on the cheek and banished from the town. Dumfries, oddly enough, was also the scene of the last public hanging in Scotland in 1868 when a simple-minded labourer was executed for rape and murder.

MID STEEPLE

Four years before the Act of Union, a windfall of 20,000 merks from the privatisation of the Customs Dues & Tacks inspired the burgh to seek a fashionable replacement for the older tolbooth which was then cautiously retained to serve as a gaol. The Building Committee engaged the services of a Liverpool architect to furnish them with plans, allegedly modelled on the college steeple of the old Glasgow University, off the High Street. One Tobias Bachup of Alloa, a master mason recommended by Sir William Bruce, Architect Royal, was appointed to implement the building of the mid steeple as the new tolbooth came to be called. Sited within the old marketplace, long and narrow in plan and built in local red sandstone, it is three stories high with a tall elegant clock tower or steeple at one end and the entrance and forestair at the other. It displays the typical classical parti of a rusticated base which housed the gaol, a piano nobile or main floor at first-floor level containing the council chamber, and an attic storey of meeting rooms, topped with a cornice and fretted balustrade. The entrance elevation has an interestingly asymmetric appearance, the forestair, with its unusual wrought-iron balustrade (by Patrick Sibbald of Edinburgh) lying across the facade, placing the entrance to one side rather than in the middle of the façade.

Early privatisation of custom dues led to the construction of a new tolbooth, the Mid Steeple

The windows are relatively regular, but a series of carved panels and cast plaques compound the asymmetry; a royal coat of arms, a low relief carved of St Michael, patron saint of the burgh, a somewhat oddly selective mileage table of the distances to Glasgow, Edinburgh, Carlisle, Huntingdon and London and a bronze relief model of the burgh at the time of Burns, all add up to an unusual richness, augmented finally by a standard ell, fixed to the wall. Inside the mid steeple porch, the ceremonial key of the clock is now displayed on the wall with a grisly notice which is a reminder that private Georgian gentility went hand in hand with a public barbarity that is almost unimaginable today. The punishment for peat stealing in the burgh was to be branded by the red-hot clock key heated on the stolen peats; no doubt again in public for the edification or entertainment of the burghers.

Is the Huntingdon reference on the mileage indicator a relic of Bruce's English title: the Earl of Huntingdon? Is this the real reason why the old Scotch drove roads stopped at Huntingdon, presumably to allow the cattle to be fattened after their long journey south? With its rusticated quoins and elegant lead cupola and weather-vane, the mid steeple certainly lives up to the committee's desire for a handsome new 'landmark' which would enhance and identify the burgh.

TRADES HOUSE

Georgian society appears to have left its mark firmly on Dumfries. The handsome Trades House of 1804 with its pedimented façade, arcaded and rusticated ground floor, is an urbane example of its kind and, with the mid steeple and earlier (1753) Queensberry Monument, forms an unforgettable sequence of buildings in the main square of the burgh. The ram's heads on the base of the column suggest the agricultural base of the town's prosperity, while the lantern at the top of the monument indicates a certain canniness (or practicality), perhaps not uncharacteristic of the 'Doon Hamers'.

The series of fine, but shabbily utilised or even flagrantly neglected Georgian town houses along Irish Street, must surely present a case for proper restoration and more elegant use of these properties; No 75 is particularly fine. From the opposite of the Nith, this expansion of the burgh along its old Back Row is quite visible and creates a powerful image with the mid steeple cupola in the background. There are other fine houses of the period in English Street and in Nith Place, and later Regency houses can be found in Castle Street, George Street and Albany Place.

At the bottom of the High Street, across the

Queensberry Monument and (below) fine
Georgian townhouses

Archibald Malcolm's townhouse: an 18th-century throwback to Renaissance styles

road in Shakespeare Street, is the town house of Archibald Malcolm, a former town clerk. Built in 1753 it is a proper little Renaissance-style palace, with a projecting centre pavilion, pedimented, with parapet urns, projecting quoins, a pedimented door entablature with a striking fanlight, and a finely carved girl's head as a keystone over the door: now Slim Jim's lounge. What a pity that Shakespeare Street beyond the neighbouring church has been ruthlessly razed by way of 'improvement'.

THEATRE ROYAL

Further up Shakespeare Street is the finest remaining Georgian theatre in Scotland, sadly now rather exposed by the traffic planners' wasteland. When the Theatre Royal was originally built in 1792, Burns was a founder member and attended the opening night. Since then, it has had a chequered career. Extended in 1830, it was converted in 1906 to a cinema with the wonderful name of the Electric Theatre which then closed in the 1950s. Re-opened as a theatre in 1960, it is the oldest working theatre in Scotland. The exterior is rather Italianate in appearance with a tripartite arched ground-floor arcade, a blank elevation to the main floor and an arcaded window range in the centre of the top floor with curious corner pilasters and a projecting cornice. Inside is a typical Georgian horseshoe-shaped proscenium theatre, designed by Thomas Boyd; originally it sported the Royal Arms on the roof. Through Robert Burns's agency, Alexander Nasmyth, the renowned landscape painter, gave his services as a scene painter, and the founder members had silver tickets.

J. M. Barrie, the author of *Peter Pan* and John Paul Jones, the father of the American Navy, who both attended Dumfries Academy, and William Paterson, founder of the Bank of England and the Bank of Scotland, as well as promoter of the ill-fated Darien scheme and even John Laurie of *Dad's Army* fame all came from or lived in Dumfries. Yet, the genius with whom it will always be associated must surely be Robert Burns.

ROBERT BURNS

Burns came to Dumfries in 1787 to look at the farm of Ellisland which his good friend and admirer in Edinburgh, Patrick Miller, had offered to lease to him on his newly acquired Dalswin Estate. The Town Council made Burns a Freeman, a Burgess of the Town, and with some reservations on its economic validity, Burns accepted Miller's offer after another Edinburgh friend Graham of Fintry, an Excise Commissioner, obtained a post for him in the Excise service, allowing him an extra income to augment his agricultural earnings.

The farm lacked a farmhouse, and Burns stayed nearby while a house was built at Ellisland to house him and his family. His landlord, Miller, employing the services of Thomas Boyd (mentioned earlier) to produce a simple, elegant, functional building.

Burns produced some of his finest work here, the immortal *Auld Lang Syne* and *John Anderson, My Jo*, here too he took part in the maiden voyage of the World's first paddle steamer.

Patrick Miller, his landlord, was an interesting man. A director of the Bank of Scotland, and of the innovative Carron Ironworks, he was keenly experimenting with application of steam power and, in partnership with William Symington, engineer at the nearby Wanlockhead lead mines, had built a prototype vessel which he tried out on Dalswinton Loch in 1788 inviting Burns and Alexander Nasmyth to join him. Later, he and Symington built the *Charlotte Dundas* which plied the Forth & Clyde Canal for some time. He was also the first man in Britain to plant swedes, a gift to him from the King of Sweden.

Burns was finally forced to give up the farm, and moved into a flat in Dumfries in a pleasantly restored Georgian town house in Bank Street, or 'Stinking Vennel' as Burns would have called it, on account of the central gutter which drained the town's fleshmarket into the Nith, a comment on the gentility of the Georgian period where elegance and squalor existed side by side.

A year or so later he moved to his final residence, a larger and more comfortable, if less elegant, house in Mill Street. Built in the local red sandstone, the house had two bedrooms, a parlour, a study and a kitchen and Burns was able to employ a maidservant. This was his

Burns' last house, now a museum complete with his favourite chair

home till his early death in 1796 at the age of thirty-seven. The house is now a museum where his favourite chair and other memorabilia are preserved.

Burn's egalitarian sympathies flourished in Dumfries, not always to his advantage. His friend Dr Maxwell had been a member of the Revolutionary Guard in France and had been present at the execution of Louis XIV, and Burns had expressed sympathy for both the American and the French Revolutions, a dangerous move in Hanovarian Society. He was accused of joining in the singing of revolutionary songs at a gala meeting in the newly built Theatre Royal, of which he was a co-founder, as he was of the new public library, and called to account and warned by his highly placed friends he must remain silent.

In this period he wrote his A man's a man for a that and Scots' Wha Hae a thinly veiled comment on the House of Hanover. His favourite howf was of course the Globe Tavern, a pleasant inn in a close off High Street, today still much as it was in Burns's day, the room where he and his friends dined and dreamed and conversed is still preserved, and some feeling of that conviviality still comes across.

ST MICHAEL'S

St Michael's Church nearby is another Georgian building associated with Burns. It was his local parish church rebuilt just at the time of the Jacobite Rising of 1745. Its building progress was delayed when Bonnie Prince Charlie had its new lead roof stripped to provide bullets for his army (in addition to imposing a fine of 20,000 merks, 2000 pairs of shoes, 200 horses and 100 carts on the town and taking the Provost and a local landowner hostage until the town paid up).

St Michael's Church contributed its lead roof to the Jacobite cause

In the graveyard there are many fine examples of controlled and decorative inscriptions. Appreciation of the decorative skill of the calligrapher is one of the pleasures of graveyard visiting, as well as the more obvious search for the historically important grave (Burns's or the Covenanting Martyrs) or the poignant epigraph. This, incidentally, was the graveyard so lovingly tended by Scott's Old Mortality.

A plaque inside indicates Burns's pew while in the graveyard, in the company of a fine selection of Covenanters' tombstones, can be found the Burns Mausoleum, built by public subscription after his death, his bones being re-interned alongside those of his wife and children. Inside, there is a fine monument by Turnerelli depicting the Muse finding Burns at the plough.

In 1818 Keats came to pay homage and when he asked a local man how to find the Mausoleum he was told 'There... amang the trees, roond wae a white tap', guidance to a visitor that still applies today.

A sombre note is struck by a mass grave of cholera victims, while the gate-posts are fine examples of the old sentry-box type from which the elders, Burns's 'unco guid', scrutinised intending communicants to assess their worthiness.

Public subscription also raised the funds later to commission another statue of Burns to grace the space in front of the Victorian Greyfriars Church, a space in which the statue has been moved about from time to time to make way for traffic. This provokes comment on the values of contemporary society which approves the demolition of many fine building to make way for carparks and chain stores.

MUSEUM

Across the river, early in the new Queen's reign in 1834, the old windmill on Corbell's Hill, dating from 1750, was in a ruinous state and plans were mooted for its demolition. Thankfully, a local group decided that it might be suitably retained and used as an observatory, and a new Astronomical Society was formed to that end. Advice was taken on the necessary instruments and after much discussion it was decided to commission an astronomical camera obscura. This fine instrument, made by a Mr Morton of Kilmarnock, is now the oldest working camera obscura of its kind in the world, and today it is a splendid attraction in the town, a fine place to take an overview of the town. The observatory was also brought into use as a museum and contains a fine selection of local material. Externally, the windows were 'egyptianised' and given broad sills on which to mount telescopes; later, in 1862, the main exhibition hall was added; in 1934 it was taken over by the Town Council; and in 1975 it came into the custodianship of the Nithsdale District Council.

Walter Newal was the architect who adapted the mill for observatory use and formed the spiral stair round the old mill drive-shaft. In 1841 the little temple at the side sheltering the statue of 'Old Mortality' and his pony was built, more recently glazed in to protect the monument, and in the taking up of the grounds a number of commemorative stones from demolished buildings have been made into a feature on the garden stairway and path. Inside, the famous silver gun can be found. It was given by James VI of Scotland in 1617 to the Incorporated Trades of the town to be competed for annually by shooting. Originally a little cannon, it was modified many years ago into the miniature musket it appears today.

It came into the town's possession in 1852 when the Incorporations' monopoly powers were removed by act of Parliament and their Trades House sold only fifty years after it was built. The remainder of their treasure was sold at public auction two years later - a sad end to a proud burgess tradition.

Dumfries exhibits this self-destructive mania from time to time, much of the town centre having been demolished and rebuilt over recent years. Traffic is now fortunately being restricted; and the burgh centre is now 'pedestrianised'; a shopping precinct has been created, sadly paved in anglified brick rather than in the traditional setts or Caithness slabs. One good aspect of the unified paved surface, however, is an appreciation of the original ridge in the marsh, now visible as a series of truncating undulations along the high street.

The Georgian contribution, substantial in places, gives Dumfries a pleasant, small-town character and one which could and should be strengthened by timely conservation. A step in the right direction has been taken by the re-erection of the Queensberry Monument on its original town-centre site, and makes one hope that the closing-off of the square might complete the pedestrianisation and give the burgh back its heart.

Unfortunately the sensitivity needed to do the job properly is not shown by the indiscriminate use of inappropriate catalogue 'period style' lights, bollards, and waste paper baskets (was there ever a Georgian waste paper basket?). Any further loss of genuine period buildings of fine quality should and can be resisted and the tendency to pander to 'Disneyland', visible in some of the new shopping centres, must be resisted.

The Victorians added gutsy buildings to Dumfries of sufficient dignity and character to enhance rather than demean the town. These are mostly executed with conviction in the local stone which contrasts with the rendered façades of the previous era. David Rhind's Court House of 1866 is a fine example of Victorian baronial, vigorous and consistent in its mass and in its detailing, and looks particularly well from the old bridge where its bulk towers over the north end of the town like some genuine old castle.

Greyfriars Church (1867)

CHURCHES

There was a proliferation of churches in the Victorian era, partly as a result of the disruption in 1843, and partly because of the need to rebuild dilapidated older buildings. Greyfriars, with its 147 foot steeple, built in 1867, by the Edinburgh architect, Starforth, replaced a decayed Georgian church. It impressively terminates the High Street to the north, its octagonal apsidal-end pleasingly turning the street towards the Edinburgh road and the academy.

St Mary's Church in English Street stands on the site of the former Chrystal Chapel, created by Robert Bruce's sister, Christina, in memory of her husband, Sir Christopher Seton, slain in revenge by the pro-Comyn faction.

The Victorian anti-burger chapel in Loveburn Street has a well-composed front showing a skilful use of simple repetitive elements but in these ungodly times it is now an extension of the Ewart Library.

The Free Church in George Street has an exuberantly detailed street façade. The Victorians were good at façades, inheritors of a long tradition, and, building at a rate which generated frequent opportunity, they were not afraid to experiment and adapt and were always sensitive to the opportunities of place. The collection of taller shops and offices round Church Place shows this ability to exploit styles and materials such as cast-iron in innovatory and exciting ways.

The commercial building at the corner of Greyfriars Place, with a fine cast-iron arcaded ground floor and an elegant cast-iron balcony front above, was the Free Norwegian headquarters during the Second World War, alongside it is an even franker cast-iron pub façade under projecting bay windows. Across the road on the corner of Friars' Vennel and High Street is a very fine hardwood shopfront with extremely slender members, a tribute to the skill of Victorian shopfitters and the quality of their materials.

The growth of commercial buildings was matched or preceded by those of industry. In 1858-9 a vast new steam mill with a chimney 174 feet high was built below the town, while across the river at Troqueer more mills were built in 1866 and 1869. It was to provide access to those from Joseph Gass's new suburb of Gasstown that the 1875 suspension bridge was built, an elegant tension structure with charming cast detail. More mills were erected later. The Rosefield mills in 1887 were the most modern of their time with electric light and modern machinery. All that remains now of these buildings is the empty shell of the Troqueer mills. The vast Nithsdale mills and chimney were demolished in 1991 but the Troqueer mills had closed after the Depression, never having found a market again. What a shame no suitable use has yet been found for these striking sturdy buildings. Only hosiery manufacture survives in the town today.

Dumfries Academy educated many notable townsmen

With the railway came the need for more modern residential accommodation which spread out later in Victorian times, to the north along the Townhead and Edinburgh roads, from the rebuilt Railway Station Hotel (the Station has some charming Victorian iron fretwork on the platform and is a good way to enter Dumfries)—predominantly large red sandstone villas, turreted, bay windowed, exotic in their geometry compared to their simple Georgian predecessors. With the growth in residential accommodation and the proliferation of churches came a growth also in school facilities and the old academy was demolished and new buildings built to replace and extend facilities

ACADEMY

The academy buildings show the Victorian attitude to free-standing buildings, whether residential or, in this case, educational. This group of Victorian, Edwardian and early and later twentieth-century

buildings is a good example of how the layers of time can be expressed, while the unity of place and groupings is maintained by the use of the local red sandstone. J. M. Barrie, John Paul Jones, Robert Burns's children (free as children of a burgess) and William Paterson were all distinguished former pupils of this institution, which dates its recorded history back to at least 1481 when the Rector, Patrick Turnbull, is mentioned in the tax rolls of the burgh.

Interestingly, just down the road from the Academy, on the face of the Trustee Savings Bank, can be seen the 'stane man' as the statue of the Revd Henry Duncan, the minister of Ruthven who invented the world's first savings bank in 1810, is known.

MODERN DUMFRIES

The new St Andrew's Church is a pleasing contemporary addition

Another place where the Victorian meets the modern in a clever combination is the new Catholic St Andrew's Church which occupies the site on Castle Street of the older Victorian church which burned down in 1961. In erecting the replacement the architect, John Copland of Sutherland Dickie & Copland, opted to keep the unique, undamaged mid-nineteenth-century towers of the previous church, which formed a striking landmark in the town and the street, where they blend harmoniously with the robust County Buildings of 1893. What is clever about St Andrew's is the way the square plan of the new church is entered. Approached between the existing towers, the door is at one corner creating a long diagonal axis across the church with an interesting diagonal roof-light to match. The altar dominates the church under this top lighting.

The detailing is simple and effective and the building is a worthy twentieth-century addition to the burgh—unlike, for example, the shopping centre beyond the Globe Inn which seeks to emulate the old burgh buildings but lacks the historic verisimilitude as well as the gutsy energy and is a poor substitute for the former burghal buildings.

Paradoxically, the other shopping centre just across the High Street, is somewhat hostile and depressing on this side, but the corner tower on Shakespeare Street shows a sympathetic use of local materials but has a better presence and detailing in Irish Street. In itself it is cleanly detailed.

The crassest assault in the old town, however, must surely be the new red-brick government office block further along Irish Street, opposite a rather fine Georgian house now serving as a job centre. Erected around 1986, it is a crude brick box separated from its neighbours by car parks and yards, set back presumably against some notional widening of the street and, all in all, effortlessly destroys the unity of that whole piece of the town between High Street and Whitesands. In comparison, the two shopping centres already mentioned seem innocuous. This is an example of twentieth-century self-interest at its worst.

Functionalism, the early modern twentieth-century creed, was a belief that if the building was simply designed to meet the needs of its users, whether a school, a factory or a house, and expresses its direct use of simple

New government offices make unimaginative use of red-brick design

building materials without reference to style, then a satisfactory architectural solution would emerge. The interests of the onlooker, the demands of existing urban considerations such as a site on the corner of the town square, or in a historic street such as Irish Street, were not a part of the design equation.

This was a view inevitably rejected by the onlookers, the public, hence the reaction against the modern and the dialogue about 'carbuncles' in recent years. It is perhaps fortuitous in view of some widely expressed royal views on architecture, that here in Dumfries, in the very building in which the royals' green welly boots are made (as the Royal Warrant above the door attests), an opportunity occurs to examine this idea of functionalism a little more closely.

Adjacent to the factory is a row of simple cottages, the product of an earlier era, and of the agricultural rather than manufacturing industry. These are simple, decent buildings, the walls perforated by neatly proportioned windows and doors, the roof, a simple pitch across. The and back walls at New Abbey was similar, but slightly more ornamented by the striking ventilator over the kiln, and by the timber wheel and lade which gave it purpose. These buildings have a simple expression of purpose and function, and lie at the root of the Modern Movement.

The Gates factory alongside, now manufacturing rubber products, is a descendant of this philosophy, the direct use of materials, the simple arrangement and expression of function. It is not only a fascinating, good building in itself, it also has an interesting history. Possibly it is the first ferro-cement factory in Britain, built in 1913 to the designs of Albert Khan, an American architect who was Henry Ford's architect and built all his car factories in America.

The factory was erected for the Arrol-Johnston Company who manufactured a 15.9 bhp touring car as its basic product, and later a smaller 10.5 bhp family car and their designer, S. Keoch, designed and produced an even lighter, sportier car in his home town of Dalbeattie.

The Gates Factory is functionalism at its best

Unfortunately, the company failed in the Great Depression in 1929 and car manufacture ceased, but not before it constructed the famous Bluebird in which Sir Malcolm Campbell achieved the world's land speed record. It was later requisitioned by the Royal Air Force and an airport built nearby, and after the Second World War was taken over by the old North British Rubber Company, now Gates Rubber Company.

It is very simple, direct building, shaped by the exigencies of manufacturing rather than dwelling or milling. The wide spans needed for manufacturing machine processes are made possible by the use of the reinforced concrete frame, while the metal windows column to column, allow the necessary high level of lighting inside. Manufacturing elements such as silos and water towers can be attached where necessary and the entrance front is signalled by the signs above the door and by the vestigial cornice which raised the height along the front end, handsome tower, one bay round the side for the diagonal view as you approach the road. The office windows are subtly differentiated from those of the manufacturing area and it seems an appropriate building, logically designed for its purpose.

Just up the road, at the Penman Works (custom built cars) we see another good example, geometrically satisfactory dispersal hangars on the old airfield utilised as manufacturing units with elegantly simple glazed fronts added to the marvellous direct curved sheds supplied in haste for war.

Functional architecture and mass produced products have a lot to offer and a look at the well-designed little greenhouse in the garden directly across the road from the Gates factory shows a building of today which the owners of Georgian houses might admire and even build in their own gardens.

The problems of some more recent architecture have arisen when the contingencies of place, and even meaning or social significance, have failed to be taken into account, as the 'brick box' in Irish Street adequately and crassly demonstrates. Mostly this has been through thoughtlessness, in some instances simplistic development greed may have been a factor. Certainly we live in a very self-centred, money-oriented society now, and it may be that we get the building we both deserve and want.

Dumfries is a good example of a burgh which flourished, despite a harsh beginning, to become a prosperous market town and seems to be adapting to its role today as a regional shopping centre. Its tourist potential must make its future secure if the over-optimistic ravaging of the expansionist 1970s and 1980s can be halted. There do seem to be signs of re-awakened civic consciousness and some of the newer buildings seem to address the idea of context and seek to please the onlooker. After all, a town which has preserved a poet's pub, but allowed a prince's parlour to be destroyed, must have its own values.

III

THURSO

Fashion, Fish and Fission

The most northerly burgh on the Scottish mainland, Thurso is set within a deep bay in storm-hewn cliffs facing across the most dangerous sea passage in Britain, the Pentland (or Pictland) Firth, towards the isles of Orkney.   It lies in a vast remote landscape under enormous skies surrounded everywhere by beautiful Caithness stone, multi-coloured and easily quarried, a perfect building material.

A Norse *borg* frequently mentioned in the Viking sagas, Thurso takes its name from its situation at the mouth of Thor's river, *Thor's aa*, but the prevalence of neolithic remains all around suggest a much older origin.

So important were Thurso's established Norse trade routes in the Middle Ages, that David I decreed its weights should become the standard for all of medieval Scotland.

BURGH

From the time of its assimilation or re-integration into the Scottish kingdom in the twelfth-century, Thurso has had a relatively peaceful history, and today, despite widespread demolition in the fifties, its lengthy history and the stages of its development can be clearly seen in its monuments and buildings.

Where the brochs, duns and neolithic cairns all around testify to Thurso's antiquity, the frequent Norse place-names give witness to Norway's ninth-century colonisation of Scotland's northern provinces.   In the old Norse, *Skara-bolsather* (Scrabster), where the former medieval bishops had their castle and from where the ferry leaves for Orkney, means 'the homestead on the cliffs' recording accurately both the character of the Caithness coast and the former Scandinavian presence.

The Norse, the Picts and Scots all fought over this land in earlier and bloodier times.   King Duncan I, who later fell victim to Macbeth, lost his nephew Moddan in a battle here in 1040 during Earl Thorfinn's successful campaign of conquest which secured to the Norse Crown all northern Scotland as far down as Moray.   On a hill above the castle a prominent monument commemorates Earl Harald of Orkney, defeated and killed here in 1196 by Earl Harald Madudson, who, five years later, returned to capture Thurso Castle and seize and torture Bishop John of Caithness. In the following century John, Earl of Orkney was murdered in the cellar of a house where he had hidden, and more importantly, at nearby Murkle, (Norse, *Myrr Kelha*, well on the moor), Earl John of Caithness (there seems to be a shortage of first names among Earls) swore fealty in 1297 to Edward I, that ubiquitous Hammer of the Scots, who certainly seems to have got around most of Scotland in his time, asserting his claims to overlordship the hard way.

After a final violent upsurge in the thirteenth century when the local farmers of *Ha Kirkia* (Halkirk) roasted the then bishop over his own kitchen fire in protest against his excessive taxation, Thurso seems to have remained relatively peaceful, the major theatre of war having shifted southwards to the Borders with the start of the Wars of Independence.

The early burgh was essentially a port, a fishing town and trading centre situated on a triangular headland on the north-west bank of the river.   The bishop's castle stood above the town on the site of an older prehistoric fort, on a little headland in the clifftops, overlooking the wide sweep of Thurso Bay and the safe anchorage of the Scrabster Roads.

A road led from the castle down into the town where the houses huddled together for shelter against the violent storms for which this coast is famous.   The high kirk, or parish church of St Peter, dedicated to the patron saint of fishermen, stood immediately above the harbour while the tolbooth and the market with its cross, were midway up the hill near to where the Victorian Town Hall now stands. There was no bridge then, nor was one built until 1800, so that the burgh remained firmly centred on the port for most of its history.   River crossings were by cobble and the ferry-men, employees of the burgh were originally employed only on Sundays.

Douneray necessitated a housing boom in the 50s and 60s

Over the centuries, the town prospered and grew and its development can be seen to divide into three distinct phases. In the first, from the eleventh to the seventeenth-century, the town was a bishop's burgh, a fishing port and trading centre dealing in corn, beef and hides, cod, herring and ling (salt fish), conducting a vigorous trade with Scandinavia. The second from around 1790 to 1910 saw the start of a consciously planned rebuilding of the town; laid out along rational lines by Sir John Sinclair of Ulbster, the feudal superior, the plan provided a useful framework for building and development until about 1920. The third phase from 1920 to the present day covers two periods of post-world war development reaching a peak with the sudden housing expansion brought about by the siting of the Dounreay power station nearby when the population rose from 3224 in 1951 to 8726 in 1961.

FIRST PHASE: EARLY BURGH

Thurso was originally a bishops' town, the Bishops of Caithness having established one of their castles there. Little can now be seen of the medieval castle sited above the town other than a grass-covered mound of ruined stone walls, but along the clifftop walk to the castle a coastguard look-out and a little private mausoleum will be found, and splendid views of Orkney enjoyed. Dunnet Head to the east is the most northerly point on the British mainland and on Holborn Head to the west, Scrabster House and Scrabster Lighthouse can both be seen, the latter designed by Robert Louis Stevenson's cousins (his own father and grandfather were also lighthouse builders). A prehistoric fort can also still be found at the very tip of the headland.

The focus of the first burgh was old St Peter's Church, down at the harbour, where the 'fisherbiggins', or fishermen's houses, were to

The Old St Peter's Church

Gable of Lod Parish Church

be found along the River Gait and the Harbour wall. The apsidal room below the tower in the now evocative ruin of St Peter's was probably the original church built at about the same time as St Margaret's Chapel in Edinburgh. The tower above was added later, in the sixteenth-century when St Peter's was much altered. In the seventeenth-century, laird's lofts were also added, and the elevations 'improved', i.e. the windows enlarged. The south gable still has fashionable gothic tracery from that time, looking surprisingly modern today and a loft front can be seen preserved in the newer St Peter's in the square.

Three and a half miles away along the road west at Crosskirk the ruin of the twelfth-century St Mary's Chapel gives some idea of what St Peter's might have been like. This church is typical of a group of chancelled churches found in Norse-occupied Caithness.

The apse was at the east end of the medieval church, which latterly and somewhat unusually had five doors: the original porch, the town's aisle door, the choir (or east) door and the school and the Earl's doors. It stood within its own kirkyard, where many fine gravestones still exist despite apparent recent neglect. It remained in use as a place of worship until 1832 when the new St Peter's was opened.

After the collapse of the medieval tolbooth, the tower and vault of St Peter's were pressed into use by the burgh as a gaol and Council Chambers, until continuing decay led to the building of a new town hall in 1871. The art of the blacksmith can be enjoyed here, in the fine Georgian railings of the graveyard and the nearby contemporary weathervane in the form of a full-rigged ship.

Fisherbiggins

From the church, Water Gait led down to River Gait and the Harbour, it was on River Gait that McAllister, an Irish pirate or freebooter was ambushed and killed with all his men when he attempted to raid Thurso on a Sunday in 1649. In the nineteenth century, the area round about the church was nicknamed Graves End, a pun on the number of Gravesend fishing smacks habitually found in the Harbour as well as on its location adjacent to the graveyard.

Thurso became a Burgh of Barony in 1633, erected in favour of the Earl of Caithness, and his grandson and heir the Master of

Berriedale. They had built a new castle at the harbour mouth some three years before where it was said gentlemen of the castle could fish from its windows. Later it was acquired by Campbell of Glenorchy who sold it in 1719 to the Sinclairs of Ulbster. That castle was demolished and rebuilt in 1872 and it is the ruins of that rebuilding we see today at the harbour mouth. The Sinclair family still live in the white house abutting onto the ruins.

So much of the old town has been swept away in recent years, it is hard to get a feeling for what it might have been like when Neil Gunn described Thurso as 'a charming town with a fishing quarter of intricate design and a building up of roofs that, seen from the beach, has a certain attraction' Several older houses can still be found among the obvious local authority housing, the oldest of any consequence being 16-18 Shore Street. Dated 1687 on a commemorative stone, its ancient neighbours have been demolished and replaced by present-day council houses, which, though paying lip

Council housing in the Fisher Town

service to the historical site in their use of material, neverthless have standard plans and elevations. This old house with its massive turnpike stair, thick walls and fascinating random façade prompts a rueful observation on our British way of doing things today.

It would be quite unthinkable in any civilised country on the Continent that a place as full of buildings of character as this was - some of them 400 years old - would be torn down to be replaced by new buildings just to ensure that a bureaucrat could check that modern minimal space standards or lighting levels or space between building standards were met; heaven forbid that somebody might be able to see in someone else's window!

The idea that such a place might be pleasant to live in, or that the houses would be different, have more character than present-day brick boxes, or might even be real and not pastiche historical buildings, is rarely taken into account. We often seem more obsessed nowadays with promoting what are often arbitrary minimum standards rather than seeking to exploit and maximise creative opportunities to enrich our environment.

Further examples of interesting older houses can be found along Riverside Drive, the former River Gait, and behind Rotterdam Street, where at least two fifteenth or sixteenth-century houses sadly look on to the unsightly guddle of superstores, car parks and derelict buildings which constitute this part of town. Eighteenth-century buildings become more frequent as you move up Shore Street, High Street and Durness Street, and also along Olrig Street, where houses of the early Georgian era can be found and recognised by their symmetry. These are built largely in stone, but some have been painted as circumstances and the owners' tastes dictate.

In a predominantly stone-built town such as Thurso occasional painted buildings add sparkle and relief, something planners don't always appreciate, in their desire for conformity. Two charming eighteenth-century houses in particular can be seen in Olrig Street, painted in vernacular colours in a very traditional way, the colour emphasising the architectural features of the buildings, their inband-outband corners and window and door surrounds.

Round the corner in Bank Street is an example of a different way of doing things, a modern abstract mural painting, a self-conscious 'artistic' contribution to the town, decorating the gable of Tollemache House, a shopping and office development named after Sir George Tollemache Sinclair, a former burgh superior. One might wonder how different this gable is from an advertising hoarding; some people might even prefer that, as they do TV commercials.

Those who prefer their art to be representative will no doubt enjoy the painted cat to be found on a low wall in nearby Pentland Crescent.

Pennyland Farm to the west of the town, is a late eighteenth-century farmhouse, famous now as the birth-place of Sir William Smith (1854-1914), who founded the Boys Brigade movement in 1883. However this stone-built farmhouse and steading also form a fine straightforward example of a type seen all round Scotland, built to a general pattern, instruments of the scientific farming that was replacing the centuries-old runrig system. Pennyland is solidly built in Caithness rubble walling with dressed ashlar margins on the house and roofed with Caithness stone slates.

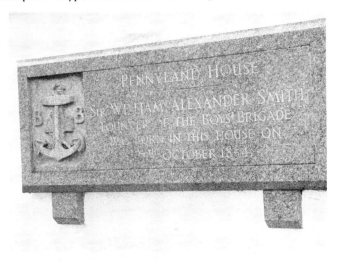

Plaque at
Pennyland Farm

More eighteenth-century houses can be found at No 5 Market Street and in Riverside Road where the former White House was the Church of Scotland manse until 1770 when it removed to Pennyland House. In Norse times land was classified for tax purposes as Monklands, Duncelands and Pennylands.

SECOND PHASE: NEW TOWN

Around the end of the eighteenth-century and the beginning of the next, things changed dramatically in Thurso. Following the 'pacification' of the Highlands after the 1745 Jacobite Rising, and in consequence of the flow of wealth from the Act of Union, a wave of 'new town' building swept over all Scotland, starting in Edinburgh. Often linked with improvement in farming, it is not surprising that Sir John Sinclair, the first president of the Board of Agriculture (1798), should want to build a new town adjacent to the old burgh of which he was the Superior.

His plan had all the clarity of the Enlightenment: a national grid-bridge and a cross-axis extending the old High Street, then continuing southwards towards the village of Hallkirk (where the early bishop was roasted or boiled in butter). Sir John laid out Hallkirk on a similar grid-iron but the village houses were smaller and the plots more spacious, clearly aiming at agricultural self-sufficiency.

A fascinating character from Scottish history, Sir John Sinclair (1754-1835) - 'Agricultural Sir John', as he was known to his contemporaries–Thurso's most distinguished native son. Born in the castle in 1754, he inherited great wealth at the age of sixteen, became a Member of Parliament at twenty-six, and a Baronet at thirty-four. Member of Parliament for the county for thirty-one, years he was a passionate improver, re-organising his estates, his town and a nearby village.

As president, also, of the British Wool Society he was responsible for introducing the Great Cheviot sheep into Caithness but, unlike many of his neighbouring lairds, he never put sheep before men and wrote wisely about how they could be introduced and incomes raised all round, through policies he had practised himself. Unfortunately, human fallibility and avid greed brought the Highland clearances in the wake of sheep, and left a legacy of bitter memories. Sir John was responsible for devising the first statistical account of Scotland and also raised his own regiment, the Rothesay & Caithness Fencibles.

His town plan was not only geometric in its layout but rational in its distribution of parts, The new town hall was to front the central square midway up the hill, seen from the approach along the new bridge; it was to be a prominent landmark, a statement of progress. As things turned out, it was built in the old town but the new St Peter's with its 140 foot tower performs the role admirably.

The cross-axis was also rationally established: Sinclair Street continues Traill or Rotterdam Street southwards linking old and new town firmly. It is now terminated by a Boys' Institute, the Miller Institute, donated by the Revd Alexander Miller of Thurso, who was the then Free Church Minister of Buckie. It cost £1500 in 1859 and has a tetra-style Roman Doric portico and a rather individual clock

The Miller Institute donated by a local clergyman

tower with cupola over. Built with a front elevation of polished ashlar and dressed rubble sides and rear, it graces the town at the end of its long street. Formerly it was entered, oddly, from river front Janet Street up a long side-on drive enclosed by walls.

The pride of place in new Thurso, must go to Janet Street, (Sir John's mother and wife were both called Janet so he could hardly be accused favouritism in so naming it). This street of linked Georgian houses offers a fascinating set of architectural variations on a theme. The houses all seem to have simple front elevation. The door is in the centre, a window on either side and above the door, just as in the classic child's drawing of a house. On closer inspection, however, each house proves to be subtly different from its neighbours. Dating from 1800 to 1810 these wide-front, three-bay, two-storey houses are faced in tooled ashlar and employ a variety of classical architectural devices, fanlights, roundels, rusticated coins, Venetian windows (sometimes with blind side windows) presenting a unique, personalised, facade to the street, while maintaining a simple unity as a totality.

Even the later Thurso Club at the top end, Victorian and vigorous but coarse by comparison with the earlier simpler but elegant houses, is still recognisable as a variation on the street theme. It has two bay windows and a rusticated base and a mock balustrade over the door. Janet Street offers a wonderful lesson in harmony and in rhythm.

Georgian doorway in Janet Street

Georgian architecture, in essence, was very straightforward, a matter of simple symmetrical elevations, with clear differentiation between the front and the back, the public and private aspects of the building. Good manners normally demanded the front should face and enhance the street and the back be decently concealed.

An unusual house which breaks these rules can be found on the corner of Paterson's Lane and Barrock Street where the architect or builder has taken advantage of the possibility of side entry from the lane to face the house into the garden, turning the front to the back and the back to the street. But the interest in symmetry persists and two blind windows have been introduced in the street elevation to make it symmetrical. The pity is that it is the only harled elevation in a street of stone.

Incidentally, a stroll round the new town will reveal a variety of blind windows of all types and even blind doors - confirmation of the desire for symmetry and the wish to please the onlooker. It will also belie the belief of the American amateur architect President Thomas Jefferson, who believed the grid-iron plan was democratic and anti-hierarchical, and its adoption in the New World would lead to the elimination of social distinction. In Thurso it does not seem to have quite worked out that way: the grand houses are on riverfront Janet Street facing the Mall and Park, while at the top of the hill the houses are much smaller and less pretentious.

A house in the New Town

SQUARE

The new town square, too, developed slightly differently from Sir John's original intentions in that the proposed resiting of the town hall never happened, and

instead, in 1832, a new St Peter's Church was built to overlook the gardens where a fine commemorative statue (1835) of Sir John, by Francis Chantry of London, stands today in Sinclair Square, moved there from its original site in the castle when Sir Tollemache Sinclair gifted it and the gardens to the town in memory of his famous grandfather.

The church is vaguely perpendicular English gothic in style, crowned by a display of a multitude of pinnacles and a tall tower with a clock with three faces, as well as a pointed gothic porch at the front. The interior, seating up to 1500, has a balcony supported on Roman Doric cast-iron columns and a gothic pulpit, undoubtedly a church built in the age of eclecticism.

A local anecdote is told of the church clock, gifted to the town by a John Miller of London. In the latter years of the last century this clock's face was illuminated and served the town well, maybe too well. On one occasion at least a group of boisterous revellers set the hands back an hour, in the hope of

St Peter's Church.

*Scottish
Episcopal
Church*

persuading a local landlady that she was calling 'Time, gentlemen please', an hour too early. It worked too, it seems.

A little further along Sinclair Street the rather typical but undistinguished 1960s telephone exchange is built on the site of the old legal stamp office presided over a hundred years ago by Miss Jeannie Sinclair who, for a short period of time, served her customers wearing pink satin stays over her dress.

'They're really too beautiful to wear underneath',she told them. Perhaps this is where Madonna got the idea?

The west church at the corner of Sinclair Street and Robertson Lane (the east/west streets were rather narrow, and called lanes), is another landmark in the town, with a fine 110 ft spire, which can be seen to great advantage from across the river. It was built in 1859 by David Smith of Thurso and is still in use for worship. The number of churches in the town is a perverse tribute to the disputative nature of the Presbytarian church of Scotland and to the wealth of the Victorian community which erected them. Is this multitude of churches found in every Burgh, a Scottish peculiarity. One other church is noteworthy: the little church (adjacent to the Bridge), which has a round Brechin-style tower, surely a symbolic reference to Thurso's Viking past.

INDUSTRY

Sinclair's plan was functional as well as elegant and industry formed an essential part of his proposals. His drawings indicate, carefully screened from the bridge approach by a row of houses on Caithness Street (now Sir George's Street), a brewery, markets for meat, fish and fowl, and farm produce, a tan yard, a washing green, a new harbour wall—all grouped in a tidy 'service quarter'. Across the river, mill and factory buildings were also envisaged, sited to exploit water as power, as a motive force and for industrial processing.

The Youth Hostel

Possibly because these buildings faced posh Janet Street across the river, somebody had a lot of fun disguising their functional nature, by building a splendid fake castellated gothic gable with a blind pointed window. When these buildings were built in 1810, the trees across the river were not tall enough to screen these industrial buildings, hence this elaborate 'folly', putting a good face on it, in social terms.

Today the mill buildings are a very good example of creative preservation. Recently converted by the local authority to new use as a youth club and hostel, they are now ensured years of further useful life. Oddly, the same local authority which preserved the mill, now seem to be putting forward proposals to demolish the historic but somewhat dilapidated brewery buildings in Manson Lane. Not only would this be a great pity for social reasons but their removal now would be a visual disaster of the first order, immediately exposing the full squalor of the car park behind, as the first prospect of the burgh from the east. Fortunately, a group of concerned local people have come up with a proposal to use them for a creative glass-making centre, thereby preserving the town's architectural integrity and adding to its sightseeing attractions. Surely, in an age of tourism, this is a matter of sound commercial as well as social sense?

OLD TOWN CENTRE

Further up Manson Lane towards the old town centre, the little circular stone building with a conical capped roof houses the Victorian pumping mechanism of the Meadow Well, the burgh's traditional water supply.

The house of Robert Dick can be found nearby in Wilson Street. Dick, commemorated by a fine obelisk in the cemetery, was a baker by trade and a botanist and geologist by inclination. He furnished fossils to and exchanged information with Hugh Miller of Cromarty, who wrote *The Old Red Sandstone* and *Footprints of the Creator*. This was at the time when scientific theories were upsetting strongly held religious views about the creation and geologists' evidence was crucial to the arguments. The plaque on Dick's house also informs us:

> Robert Dick, Geologist and Botanist, lived here 1830-1866 earning his daily bread by hard work, obliged to read and study by night and yet able to instruct the Director General of the Geological Society.

TOWN CENTRE

Banking in the new town

The architecture of Thurso's town centre is relatively undistinguished but the Victorian part is well built in decent stone and slate and many interesting details can be found. Gables come in vernacular, Dutch and gothic styles and banks and churches abound as might be expected.

The town can probably survive the drastic twentieth-century surgery that has carved away areas of the old town, if it goes no further and if some of the more obvious recent disasters receive a more cosmetic surgery. A typical example in the pedestrian way, is the way the normal vertical emphasis has been brutally shattered by a long horizontal cantilevered gallery above recent shops, and the recent proliferation of fast-food shops and cheap stores is hardly attractive to tourists. The vast drab areas of the superstores and their car parks must receive landscape attention soon if they are not to become totally squalid.

Fanlights on the old British Linen Bank.

The Town Hall also houses a local museum

The Town Hall (1870) has a vigorous Victorian gothic elevation, enlivened by the flapping brightly coloured flags in front, and presenting some heavily modelled gabelets or dormers, stained-glass windows, and painted doors with decorative hinges. The architect, J. Russell Mackenzie of Aberdeen, gained the commission by the success of his Aberdeen Town & County Bank (now the Clydesdale) of 1866 in Traill Street (named after the landowner who started up the Caithness flag-stone industry which paved half of London and brought wealth to Victorian Thurso).

The market place in front of the Town Hall at one time housed the 'cocky stane' and the 'fish stane', as well as the jougs, the gibbet and the mercat cross. A little museum of local history inside the Town Hall will explain much and is worth a brief visit.

Further up Olrig Street on the main road to the west is St Andrew's Church, a former Free Church, and a replacement of an older church. Built in 1870 by J. Russell Mackenzie, it contains Sir George Sinclair's memorial and has a cast iron balconied interior. Now a joiner's shop its preservation is fortuitously secured at present as an important terminal to Rose Street. Externally it presents a wonderful concoction of crow-stepped gables, stained-glass tracery, towers, turrets and finials. It once had a clock and is unusual in having its apsidal end at the entrance.

Across Olrig Street a little further on, at the corner of Castle Street, is the Masonic Hall. Built as a volunteer drill hall in 1873 and noticeable for its castellated aspirations this rather striking little building is the kind of idiosyncratic ingredient which adds spice to a town. It also illustrates an interesting architectural point: its employment of battlements, turrets and arrow slots is purely decorative, symbolic rather than real, meant to inform us that it is a military building, these devices are a conscious, almost literary, expression of its character.

A genuine castle or a real atomic reactor for that matter, would convey

The Masonic Halls employ decorative military features

its nature directly through a functional expression of use, something instantly appreciated at Dounreay. Both modes of expression are architecturally legitimate and both tell us a lot about the building and the culture which produced it. The adoption of symbolic motifs as means of expression occurred widely both in the Renaissance, where architects made reference to the buildings of classic Rome and in the nineteenth century, the era of historical eclecticism and the period in which the hall was built.

Outside Thurso, approached from the A882 Wick Road via a tree-lined avenue, is a most impressive walled enclosure, the graveyard (or set of graveyards now) which took over from St Peter's old churchyard when the churchyard was full. In the new St Peter's Church ,in the wall of the graveyard, in addition to the usual upright gravestones, the visitor can find a series of unusual monuments set on the diagonal: one bears the portrait sculpture of David Smith, architect of the Masonic Hall and the West Church; another is of a lichen-covered lady holding an anchor standing on a little domed temple enclosing an urn.

Long, wordy and descriptive inscriptions seem to be a Thurso tradition, one carried on in the adjoining contemporary graveyards, which unusually seem to have been started before the

The Infirmary

David Smith's Grave

older area was anywhere nearly filled in. These are full of contemporary sandblasted granite stones sometimes bearing rather curious images in a funeral context, for its population Thurso must surely have the largest graveyards in Scotland.

A little gate at the foot of the older graveyard goes down to the river walk and a footbridge across to the Dunbar Hospital, which looks at first glance like some baronial castle. Why buildings should wish to emulate another different kind of building is a perennial question in architecture, especially relevant today when supermarkets are disguised as houses in Elgin or as rustic barns and stables in Essex.

Just down the road Sir Basil Spence's post-war Thurso High School can be distinguished from a block of flats largely by the absence of curtains on the windows, and the lack of doorways. It is nevertheless pleasantly colourful and in a well-landscaped environment, even if the *gravitas* of older public buildings is missing.

Further out of Thurso at the other end past Crosskirk and St Mary's lies the atomic power station which brought

Sir Basil Spence's High School

controversy and work to the burgh. There is no pretence about Dounreay, it is exactly what it seems: a twentieth-century industrial building, gigantic in size, utilitarian in purpose, clear in its parts, sitting fittingly in the vast bleak Caithness landscape. A visitor centre offers guided tours, no doubt to allay fears as well as to inform. An ancient castle sits inside the site incongruous among its enormous neighbours!

The nearby village of Reay also rewards a visit. It has some fine Celtic carved stones in its old graveyard, and an effectively simple black and white vernacular church on a little hill above the village. An access road leads down to a the nineteenth-century safe harbour of Sandkirk, constructed to provide shelter from the fury of the Pentland Firth. Once an export port for haematite (iron-ore) and smoked salmon it now offers a 'picturesque' view of the Dounreay Reactor across the harbour mouth. It still has its old warehouses and a fishermen's net-drying green on the headland.

The castle ruins which overlook the harbour on the east bank of the River Thurso are of a Victorian sham built between 1872 and 1875 to replace the original castle (1660) on the same site. Sir Tollemache Sinclair was then the Burgh Superior and probably planned his rather drastic renovation in anticipation of the visit in 1876 of the Prince and Princess of Wales. He entertained them to lunch on that occasion but perhaps his castle was 'jerry-built' in haste as portions of the upper battlements had to be removed for safety in the 1950s.

Returning to Thurso, out on the end of the promontory facing the ruins of Sir Tollemache's castle across the river, is a startingly white modern sewage treatment plant. Its porthole windows are reminiscent of the modern architecture of the 1940s but its streamlined shape, its simplicity and its breakwater are all in the same marine tradition of functional building as the Scrabster Lighthouse on Holborn Head across the bay. This little building its at the end of the esplanade with a breakwater to protect it from the force of winter storms at least 50 feet from the esplanade, a tribute to the power of the sea.

Thurso has a splendid beach, where a school of whales was beached in 1899 and where today surfers can often be seen, as many of the best surfing waters in Britain are to be found around here. In the mid-eighteenth century it was a punishable offence to remove stones from the beach, except for street making, and in 1882 a long protective concrete esplanade was built to protect the seaward edge of the town. The present beach apparently once offered productive cattle grazing before the encroachment of the sea, and was known as the Links of Ormlie.

Marwood Sutherland, the poet ,wrote of Thurso Bay:

> see Naples Bay the poets say
> See Naples Bay and Die
> See Thurso Bay and live for aye
> Upon its shores, says I

What gives Thurso a unique quality as a burgh and makes it memorable is the way it demonstrates the visible co-existence, side by side, of two contrasting modes of living, the clustered row houses of the fisher village and the independent yet architecturally conforming pavilions of the new town. This manifestation surely is a consequence of both culture and class, a point of view perhaps underlined by the ease with which today, the local authority housing has taken over the ethos of fishertown, and forms a similar enclosed community. The new town houses imply a desire for individuality and privacy, yet conform willingly in their architectural pretensions with a shared social perception of how a house and a town ought to look. Interesting, also, is the way these two styles of living are logically connected by the main through route and the shopping street which house most of the town's communal institutions.

This organic relationship maintained and strengthened by the Victorians is in clear contrast to the banality of later post-war housing schemes, which tend to be residential ghettos with no social facilities or landmarks, other than the odd school and a very occasional hall. Their street patterns, too, tend to be just that: patterns, rather than an expression of function.

Today, Thurso can be seen as a sort of mini Edinburgh, with its old and new towns side by side, epitomising different ways of living, together apart, as it were.

Many lessons can be learned here about the totality of town life and how it can be provided for and about issues in architecture in the past and the present, which, added to the pleasure of travel and enjoyment of the splendid views and landscapes, on arrival make a visit a worthwhile and unforgettable experience.

IV

PAISLEY

Medieval Roots and Mercantile Monuments

*Evening
Citizen
following
Glen
Cinema
Disaster*

Paisley is the home of the handkerchief, Brown & Polson's patent cornflour, Golden Shred marmalade and its famous golliwog, as well as Shanks plumbing and Dobie's Four Square tobacco tins. Famous for shawls, poets and its abbey, in time it has been a bishop's burgh, a hotbed of social and religious dissension linked with the American Revolution, and the capital of a world-wide textile empire.

It has also been the scene of two major disasters involving children: the Paisley Canal Disaster (1810) when over 100 children (mostly 12-14 year-old textile workers) drowned when a canal boat capsized, and the Glen Cinema Disaster (Hogmany 1929) in which seventy children perished in needless panic caused by smoke.

Historical figures Paisley has known include Robert Bruce, William Wallace and Walter the Steward, father of Robert II, founder of the Stuart line of kings as well as the Revd John Witherspoon who left Paisley to become Principal of Princeton and the only clergyman to sign the American Declaration of Independence. Emancipationist Harriet Beecher Stowe campaigned, Charlie Chaplin entertained, Pavlova danced, and Edmund Kean, the Regency actor, played regularly in Paisley.

The Evening C

TERRIBLE DISASTER
OVER SIXTY CHILDREN LOSE
THEIR LIVES
Crushed and Trampled Following
Terrible Panic
GRUESOME SPECTACLE MEETS EYES
OF RESCUERS
Pile of Victims Six Feet High
TRAMCARS AND 'BUSES USED AS
CONVEYANCES TO INFIRMARY
Agonised Women's Clamour and Rush
in Attempt to Identify

BURGH

Contiguous with Glasgow, Paisley seems like its larger neighbour, very much a late nineteenth-century tenement town ravished by traffic 'improvements' and littered with large, abandoned industrial buildings. Only its ancient abbey hints that there might be more to Paisley than it seems.

Dominating the 'cross' in the heart of the town is an enigmatic anachronistic statue of Robert the Bruce—not gazing proudly over the scene of some famous victory, but supporting and sheltering four kilted Scottish soldiers of the First World War. An unusual but compelling concept for a War Memorial, beautifully executed and prominently sited in the very heart of the town, Sir Robert Lorimer's statue is nevertheless in its own way a fitting metaphor for the town itself; its medieval foundation and its twentieth-century condition.

The Town Hall and the 'young mum'.

The view out from the 'cross' is equally symbolic with the dominant Gothic bulk of the abbey tower in the background, the upright classic town hall in the middle distance alongside the bridge, and, in the immediate foreground, the dignified statues of Peter and Thomas Coats, scions of the textile family and whose benefactions so enriched her architectural heritage. Modestly they gaze away into space, embarrassed perhaps by the manifest charms of a young nursing mum, herself inappropriately facing the gentlemens' loo, a dubious double confrontation of the kind to bring a smile to the face of the urban explorer.

The 'cross', as the central square is familiarly called, is clearly an ancient marketplace, its tolbooth and mercat cross long gone. The Hie Gait, or High Street, still runs west to Whitburn Abbey and the Ayrshire coast and east across the bridge over the River Cart to the abbey and to Glasgow seven miles beyond.

Originally dubbed the 'Vennelle', its new name hinting at the marshes it must have crossed, Causeyside leads out south to Kilmarnock, while Moss Street goes north under the railway to Sneddon, the town's first Georgian planned extension, built over the former cow pastures of the town's nether common.

A typical burghal pattern emerges clearly with narrow tofts stretching uphill from the Hie Gait to a Back Walk (Oakshaw Street) behind long-gone walls, and downhill to where the now culverted St Mirin Burn ran along the edge of the southern marshland.

But Paisley's origins go much further back, as the Brythonic remains on several nearby hills attest. Legend has it that in about the mid-sixth century, Mirin the Celtic Saint and Bishop established his church near a ford across the River Cart, on the Glasgow to Ayr highway, at a point where a convenient waterfall also provided the opportunity for a fishpond, an important component of any medieval community.

Naturally a little village grew up round the church. Originally called Passelat, hence Paisley, this was where later, the Benedictine monks set up their abbey Mill

and later still Peter and James Clark established their vast array of Seedhill Mills obliterating any evidence of that first settlement.

In the twelfth-century 1136 when King David I first introduced the feudal system to Scotland with its sheriffdoms and planted burghs, he granted lands in the neighbourhood and the position of Hereditary High Steward of Scotland to a certain Walter Fitz Alan, an Anglo-Norman knight of Breton origin. Walter established his castle at Renfrew to watch the River Clyde against invasion from the Gaelic kingdom of the north and south-west in particular. He established a burgh there, too, the town of Renfrew which gave its name to his new sheriffdom, Renfrewshire.

Peter and James Clark's Seedhill Mills

In 1163, as part of a wider Normanising, or as he probably saw it civilising, strategy, Walter invited Benedictine monks from the Cluniac Abbey of Wenlock, in his home lands in Shropshire, to venture northwards and establish a sister house in his new sheriffdom. The monks naturally chose a site adjacent to St Mirin's Church to found their new priory which afterwards, in 1244, became an Abbey, with the right to elect its own abbot, a rare distinction perhaps not unrelated to Paisley's later royal links.

In return for the steward's grant of lands and money the monks assisted in his administration of the shire, with the scientific farming of his lands and in the introduction of civilised standards of behaviour and education. In time they adopted their new country and became Scots enough to have their abbey burned during an English invasion of 1307 in retaliation for Sir William Wallace's depredations.

A year after the Battle of Bannockburn (1314) Walter married Bruce's daughter Marjorie, founding through their son the line of Stewart kings who ruled Scotland and later England and Great Britain for the next 300 years. Marjorie died in childbirth after a fall from her horse on the Renfrew Road where today a simple cairn monument commemorates the event.

Robert Bruce had received absolution in Paisley Abbey for this part in the murder of the 'Red' Comyn. The royal connection continued when Paisley became a burgh in consequence of a papal absolution publicly granted in 1388 by the Abbot George Schaw to James III absolving him from implication of the murder of his father. By way of a quid pro quo later that year the new king erected Paisley to a Burgh of Barony in the Abbot's favour .

Incidentally, it was during the subsequent rebuilding of the abbey that Paisley acquired its magnificent fourteenth-century sewer, the finest remaining medieval drain in Britain, a curious relic in a town which did not have a proper sewage plant till 1953.

Paisley grew slowly at first, fighting off the competition of the resentful older burgh of Renfrew, which, seeking to maintain its seniority and authority, on one occasion at least mounted a midnight expedition to overthrow Paisley's new market cross. Paisley naturally retaliated and rivalry grew. However, the power of the church prevailed and James IV wrote irately to Renfrew demanding they cease harassing his new Burgh of Barony (1488) thereby allowing Paisley's development to continue.

In 1491 Abbot Schaw made a gift of a tolbooth, to his new burgh confirming its status, and increasingly the knowledge base of abbey and its encouragement of the crafts enabled the burgh to prosper and tilted the scales of fortune in Paisley's favour.

By the end of the fifteenth century Paisley had five gates or ports. The West Port was at what is now the corner of Storie Street and High Street, the Brig Port, on the west bank of the Cart, stood at the end of the bridge which by that time had replaced the ford. The south gate, St Mirin's Port, lay at the foot of St Mirin's Wynd which left the cross at a diagonal towards where St Mirin's Burn met the river; this would now place it at the south-east corner of Dunn Square. There was a Moss Port on Moss Row as Moss Street was then, and a Barn Yard Port on Oakshaw at the top of what is now Meetinghouse Lane.

The seried plasters and cut back mouldings of the West Door

Little now remains of that medieval Paisley other than the nave of the abbey and the great drain. The original settlement of Passelet or Seedhills lies buried with St Mirin's Church beneath the massive bulk of the Anchor Mills. Most of the abbey, including its great mile-long boundary wall fell victim to the short-sighted cupidity of Lord Dundonald, its eighteenth-century feudal superior, who sold off the stone for building in his new suburb of Greenlaw.

ABBEY

Of the abbey itself there still remains the original thirteenth-century west front with its tripartite doorway and the fiftheenth-century decorated Gothic nave, with its curious corbelled triforium, timber roof and stone-vaulted side aisles. At the south-east corner inside can be found an an interesting transitional Norman door and a magnificent tenth-century sculptured cross recently removed there from nearby Barochan.

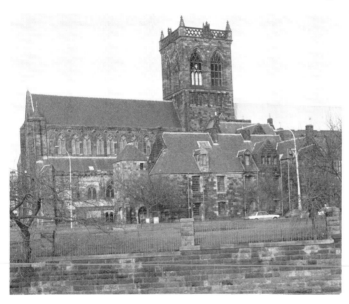

The rebuilt vaulted choir with its fine Victorian carved choir stalls and the rebuilt transepts and tower are all testimony to the vigour of Victorian and Edwardian restoration. Scholarly up to a point, sparing no expense, a tribute as much to contempory benefactors as to their architects, the building's appearance now is based on a hypothetical vision of how it might once have looked. Inside the choir a medieval recumbent female effigy adorns a burial chest reputed

The Abbey

to be that of Robert Bruce's daughter Marjorie. King Robert II, Marjorie's son and the first of the Stewart kings, is also buried there as are the first six High Stewards, his ancestors.

A fine memorial (1810) by Flaxman at the rear of the nave and a war memorial (1923) designed by Reginald Blomfield suggest Paisley continued to take pride in its great church. In 1932 Lorimer finished the choir and the rebuilding of the tower which had collapsed in 1553. He was the last of the restorers, who included James Salmon Snr. and Sir Robert Rowand Anderson among their number.

Behind the abbey is the sixteenth-century place (or palace) of Paisley. Clearly the remains of the abbey's conventual buildings, it is once again in use as the church manse having at one time been degraded to a tavern and lodging house. After the Reformation the place was much altered for his own use by Claude Hamilton, the last abbot's nephew who had been granted the title Lord Paisley and the lands of the abbey by James VI & I in reward for services to his mother, Mary Queen of Scots. James visited Paisley in 1617 and dined in the great hall of the place.

Crow-stepped Blackhall Manor on the bend of the River Cart is a sixteenth-century rebuilding of an earlier manor house established by the first steward Walter, as a hunting lodge adjacent to his abbey and its village. It has recently been restored and inhabited again.

The burgh continued to prosper after the Reformation and in 1576 it obtained a royal charter to build a grammar school to replace the monastery school. This was first built in 1586 on the south side of School Wynd and the town's first hospital followed in 1618, adjacent to the old West Port.

In 1705 the sheriff finally moved his court to Paisley in recognition of its position as the most populous and most important town in the shire.

Thus, by the time of the Union of Parliaments (1707) Paisley was securely established as an administrative and manufacturing centre of some importance. With the union came access for Scotland's merchants to a huge new market in America; indeed, this had been one of the principal Scottish motives for negotiating that agreement, and Paisley was well situated to benefit from this opportunity. Colonial America needed manufactured goods. Agricultural implements and tools, leather shoes, saddles and harnessess, and most of all, cloth and the thread to sew it with, for clothing and household linen.

Thanks to its rivers and excellent water supply Paisley had the world's first filtered water supply in 1802. Paisley had become an important weaving town specialising in linen production, a lengthy industrial process requiring considerable capital, skill, and the support of a well-developed bleaching industry. At that time weaving was essentially a cottage industry with outworkers loosely organised by a manufacturer or ('cork', as he was known locally), who supplied the raw material and marketed the finished product. When trade with America flourished, Paisley's weavers and 'corks' flourished with it.

Large amounts of capital were amassed and Paisley merchants played their part in the development of the tobacco and sugar trade in Glasgow and Greenock respectively. Paisley's weavers were skilled and well organised and earned good money, particularly in the initial days of the Atlantic trade and interesting and important links with America developed. Glassford, after whom Glassford Street in Glasgow is named, was a Paisley 'cork' who, growing rich on the cloth trade, diversified into tobacco and prospered even further. Hand-loom weaving encouraged independence, a weaver and his family were an individual manufacturing unit where a man could make cloth in his own time.

PAISLEY WEAVERS

Self-educated and articulate, the weavers had a 'guid conceit o' themsels' and tended to be radical in their politics and righteous in their religion. Disputative and divisive, prone to sectarianism, dissension and even confrontation, weavers were lively and libertarian. Their religious divisiveness is epitomised by the astonishing variety of churches in Paisley seen at its most striking along Oakshaw, where at least ten different denominational churches attest to their devotion and to the strength of their convictions.

In 1757, the Revd John Witherspoon came to Paisley's High Church. His satirical pamphlets and plays rapidly brought him into conflict with the 'corks' or employers. Successfully sued for libel he nevertheless continued to publish admonition and condemnation when he saw fit, and the offer of the post of Principal of Princeton College in America in 1766 came at a time when it was to his great advantage to accept it. Once there he became a part of American history as an adviser on the drawing up of the American Declaration of Independence and the only clergyman to sign it.

Rev John Witherspoon, signatory to the American Declaration of Independence

Liberty was in the air, and Thomas Paine's *The Rights of Man* was read everywhere. The French Revolution followed the American making the government of the day apprehensive and repressive. It sent its troops against unrest everywhere, including Paisley, but to little avail there. The well-organised textile industry gave the burghers the wealth and strength to resist any attempts to subdue them.

Their libertarian tendencies showed up in another way. In the wake of Robert Burns, poets proliferated among the Paisley weavers, the best known of whom was Robert Tannahill (1774-1810). As one of them, John Kent, neatly put it,

> Yet Paisley's name is widely spread
> History doth show it
> Been famed alike for shawls and thread
> For poverty and poets

An admirer of Robert Burns, he founded the Paisley Burns Club, which still continues to meet in his 11 Queen Street cottage, the last thatched house preserved in the town. A hand weaver, he kept his writing instruments and flute beside his loom to write his songs and poems and play as the spirit took him. Sadly he drowned himself in a fit of depression at the age of thirty-six having been rejected by his publisher and his love. Perhaps with his poet's intuition he saw that with the coming of factory weaving the days of the independent craftsman weaver were at an end.

One of Tannahill's friends, another poet and satirist, Alexander Wilson (1766-1813), exiled himself to America to escape prosecution and became America's first significant ornithologist, writing and illustrating *America's Birds* and influencing the later and more famous Audubon.

John Wilson (1785-1854) was for many years the 'Christopher North' of Edinburgh's *Blackwood's Magazine* and became Professor of Moral Philosophy at Edinburgh University.

Paisley's dissenting ministers, weavers and poets no doubt have left a little of the iron in their soul, as a characteristic of the Paisley 'buddie' (body).

Of historical importance, also, the weavers left the world the Paisley pattern, as it is now known, despite the fact that it originated in the form of imported cashmere (Kashmir) shawls, and was later copied in France and in Edinburgh and Norwich before its sophisticated development in Paisley. These shawls were used as ladies' coats during the era of the crinoline and bustle when a normal coat was precluded by fashion. Paisley's rise to international pre-eminence in shawl weaving arose out of the superior technical skill of its weavers, a judicious importation from France of the Jacquard loom and an ability to print complex patterns on linen. Paisley Museum, Art Gallery & Library, High Street, has a splendid room devoted to the shawls, the weavers and their ethos, the looms, and relics of their propensity to rebellion and free speech.

South door of High Church

Some idea of the appearance of the burgh in the late seventeenth and early eighteenth centuries can be obtained by looking up nearby West Brae, where it meets the High Street, though it is a pity that the crude fascia of the High Street shop turns the corner to destroy the illusion of the past.

A small row of one and two-storey houses in Williams Street, Robert Tannahill's thatched cottage in Queen Street built about 1750 and the 'Sma Shott' cottages in Shuttle Street all convey similar impressions. These latter are a rebuilt Victorian weavers' row recently altered to form an interesting museum with working looms.

Of interest in St George's Place, alongside the cottages, is a splendid Georgian house with a fine external stair. This was the home of a contemporary bailie and shows clearly the gap between the social level of the 'cork' and weaver living side by side in the town.

OAKSHAW

Oakshaw is the northern side of the old burgh. The original toft boundaries can still be discerned but Oakshaw's sense of place lies in its dramatic silhouette created by

the finest collection of urban monuments anywhere in the region. The High Church (1750-6) with its spectacular stepped steeple and fine baroque north door, stands at the top of Church Hill. It was designed by John White, a local bailie who was also the architect of the tolbooth. Below it is the rather plain second grammar school (1802) and the Middle Church (1779-81), a pleasant Renaissance church with a fine pedimented porch and parapet urns.

Off Church Hill along School Wynd, now authentically resetted, can be seen the Congregational Church of 1887 and, ahead, St John's Church (1862-3) by James Salmon & Son. Both these Victorian churches, so typical of the period, are fine

The High Church steeple

examples of polychromatic Revival gothic - a tribute to Ruskin's persuasive imagery.

Ahead, to the left, at the top of Meeting House Lane is the old United Free Church, classical in style with an old overgrown graveyard to one side. Behind the High Church is an extremely plain Gaelic chapel (1739) (its nameplate paradoxically in English and Latin), while further along at the far end of Oakshaw Street at the top of Westbrae lies the old Cameronian (Covenanters) Meeting Hall (1810), now converted to flats.

Midway up the hill is yet another Victorian church, Romanesque Revival this time, the Orr Square Church (1845) with two fine Georgian houses (1815) alongside.

The Gaelic chapel

COATS OF PAISLEY

Thomas Coats Memorial Church

Last, but certainly not least, is the *tour de force* of Paisley churches, the Thomas Coats Memorial, an enormous gothic Revival Baptist church standing on a giant flight of steps (concealing an undercroft of halls and meeting rooms) facing the mills whose product made its founding possible.

Coats is a name synonymous with thread and with Paisley. From small beginnings the Coats family eliminated or took over all the other thread and weaving manufacturers: the Carliles, the Kerrs and eventually even the Clarks of Seedhill (1889) (whose old head office in Well Street has a wonderfully explicit carved panel depicting a pound sign inside a wreath of thread). Coats built up a world empire of thread making Paisley its capital, and the magnificent Thomas Coats Memorial Church, its cathedral,

Carved Panel above doorway of Thomas G. Coats Memorial Church

terminates and dominates the western prospect of Paisley's High Street much as the Coats themselves dominated its economy.

Those vast front steps previously alluded to, provided not only a base for the church to stand on but a place to be seen. What a background for the Sunday church parade! Curiously enough Thomas Coats himself was wheelchair-

bound and could not have used the steps.

The biggest Baptist church in Europe, it took ten years build (1885-94). It is 165 feet long and 100 feet wide and seats 1000 people. Built of red sandstone with flying buttresses and elaborate carving, its 240 foot high tower is capped with a crown spire like that of the High Kirk of St Giles in Edinburgh. Inside no expense was spared, marble and alabaster, stone and oak, carved and fretted, abound everywhere and in the vestry is perhaps the finest Victorian lavatory to be seen in Scotland, certainly exotic for a clergyman. Over the staircase leading down to the halls below can be seen the gilded monograms of all the sons and daughters of Thomas Coats (1809-83).

No local Paisley architect was entrusted with this testimony to faith and fortune; only the best available from Edinburgh would do, with the wonderful name of Hippolyte J. Blanc (his name can be seen carved in stone below the cornice where the nave meets the east transept).

In their day the Victorian Coats were great patrons and benefactors to the town, gifting Paisley its library, its museum and observatory as well as a wealth of minor institutions, parks and statues. They had a pride in and a commitment to their native town which sadly today seems to have gone, submerged by a concern for cost. Coats thread is now manufactured in the third world in pursuit of lower costs and higher profit and Paisley has withered accordingly.

Must profit be the only criterion in our present-day society? Is money's only function to make money? Are people redundant except as units of consumption? Will that pride of place which made towns such as Paisley unique ever return?

These are difficult questions to answer yet an answer must be found if a decent modern architecture is to be left as a mark of our time. One need only look at the dreary Piazza Shopping Centre (1968-70) actually built over the river, to see how desperately we need some answers.

On Oakshaw, the social order in the eighteenth and nineteenth- centuries, the aspirations of the craftsmen weavers and the ostentatious munificence of the later textile barons can all be read in a fascinating testimony of stone. What do we read of ourselves in the Piazza today?

The contrast between the relatively sober buildings of the dissenting churches and the grandeur of those of the captains of industry is accentuated on Oakshaw by the additional monuments created in a series of splendid public benefactions, the museum and library, the observatory, the John Neilson Institution, even, as a monument to the suppression of internal dissension, the Territorial Drill Hall, a reminder that eighteenth and nineteenth-century regiment raising was directed as much against the perceived enemy within (the libertarians), as those without (Napoleon and the French, or later, the Kaiser and the Germans). Paisley had the distinction of raising the first yeomanry in Scotland, an accolade perhaps not unrelated to the articulate independence of its weavers.

John Honeyman's Paisley Museum (1868-1881), in the High Street, is entered via an austerely classical portico which gives no hint of the unexpectedly splendid staircase which climbs the hill, giving access to a series of terraced top-lit galleries (some now darkened in response to changing methods of display). A simple introduction to the history of the town is displayed in an attractive top-lit hall with an interesting iron roof-truss, the anthemion on its cast-iron compression strut a contemporary Victorian gesture to 'high tech' classicism.

Paisley Museum with its classical Ionic portico

Beyond the first gallery a wonderful long view up the stair is obtained to a circular, top-lit upper hall which cleverly conceals the changing orientation of the upper galleries to suit the site. Sheer visual serendipity and a clue as to why Honeyman's office might have attracted Charles Rennie Mackintosh.

Above the museum, entered from Oakshaw Street is another Honeyman building, a marvellously simple but grandly monumental observatory (1883), a last gift to the town of Thomas Coats. Built on a site purchased by Peter Coats for the museum extension, the observatory has a wonderful scale, the great Doric cornice with a frieze of round windows is particularly skilful. Now an observatory, weather station and seismic centre, it houses a little space travel museum and a fine old library. Inside are some intriguing stained-glass windows depicting the great astronomers. The walls of the central space house a unique ramp within their depth to accommodate Thomas Coats and his wheelchair. Sadly he was too ill to attend the opening and died

two weeks later. Originally owned by the Philosophical Society it is now organised by the local authority.

Honeyman's Ionic portico

At the end of Oakshaw Street, on the reputed site of a Roman fort is the John Neilson Institution (1849-52), whose marvellous profile forms a wonderful termination to the architectural sequence of domes and spires along the hill crest. Neilson was the man who, by inventing the blast furnace, enabled Scotland to gain early industrial success through the exploitation of the easily available Lanarkshire and Ayrshire coal and local iron-ore.

Designed by Charles Wilson, of Park Circus fame, the Institution has a cruciform plan round an octagonal hall, topped by a splendid inverted 'porridge bowl' as the natives refer to it. No longer used as a school, its future seems secured by conversion to flats, but what a pity a more significant use could not have been found for this fine, public and monumental structure.

On Oakshaw that other phenomenon, Georgian infill within the walls, can be clearly seen and some of the best Georgian domestic architecture in the town is found there. As well as the two Georgian houses in Orr Square, Oakshaw Street itself has a fine variety of villas with an odd tenement interspersed here and there. Enough remains to give an idea of what 'living on the hill' at one time must have been like.

Below Church Hill, on the other side of High Street, New Street runs downhill past the Laigh Kirk, crossing Causeyside to level out and meet the river as Orchard

Street. As its name suggests, New Street was constructed by the burgh in 1790 to finance the building of a church within its boundary and belonging to it. Previously the only church had been the nave of the abbey across the river, situated on land owned by Lord Dundonald. By feuing off tofts along this new thoroughfare the burgh raised a sum of money and an income to build and support its own church the Laigh Kirk (and furthered a little private property investment).

The other churches already mentioned followed on Oakshaw, the splendid Renaissance High Church at the top of Church Hill and then the Middle Church, either half way up or down the hill like the Duke of York's army, as you please.

Through the offices of the Paisley man who was Regent Morton's Chaplain, the Burgh had obtained a Royal Charter in 1576 to erect a grammar school. No longer evident, it is known to have been erected ten years after the Charter, on the south side of School Wynd. A third grammar school building was burned down a few years ago, the front walls in Victorian Tudor still picturesquely standing on Oakshaw Hill.

BEYOND THE BURGH

In the eighteenth-century development within and beyond the walls increasingly took place. The burgh laid out a new residential area in Sneddon to the north and the Earl of Abercon erected a second bridge across the Cart to his own planned new town, despite the protests of the guildry who feared a loss of trade and feu income to the burgh.

Greenlaw House

The outlying weavers had previously been encouraged to move into or closer to

Paisley and several new weaving villages had been laid out, Maxwellton in the west, Williamsburgh in the east and Charleston, or the 'Republic' as it was known, to the south. The town was growing in size and status. Paisley was no longer a village but with the success of trade with America a thriving, expanding town on the verge of the industrial revolution.

Greenlaw House (1774) was the home of Richard Corse, a tobacco merchant, in Mansionhouse Road, despite the disruptive but not unskillful addition of a Victorian porch, gives some idea of how splendid the new town might have been. In a nearby garden, its 'Gothick' coach house still stands in good condition, missing only its clock and original doors.

Most of this area was developed much later in Victoria's time onwards and several intriguing specimens of the 'villa' genre can be found. A curious pair of terraced houses can also be found immediately adjacent, with fascinating precast concrete decorative parts, columns and balusters and extraordinary dormers with arts and crafts 'sunbursts'.

INDUSTRIAL PAISLEY

An important consequence of the discovery and spread of steam power in industry was that resources were increasingly concentrated in fewer and fewer hands. Weaving ceased to be a cottage affair, and manufacturing was increasingly carried on in purpose built factories. After the 1840s an adequate life for the independent weaver was impossible.

In 1782 a steam-powered cotton factory was built in Paisley, the fourth in Scotland (the first two were in Glasgow, the third in nearby Barrhead), with engineering support for the new mechanical weaving industry rapidly established. Weaving more or less ceased to be

Classical villas in pre-cast concrete

craft based and, as Paisley's range of technological expertise and skills widened, engineering came to the forefront.

By 1733 there were ninety-three thread mills and by the 1780s the steam mills were making thread from cotton instead of from more expensive linen. By the 1860s there were only four families left in textile production outside the big three (Kerr, Clark and Coats). Clark's mills were at Seedhill, the original site of the abbey's mills across the river from an earlier Georgian mill now converted to a hotel, while the Coats, interested only in thread, built their mills at Ferguslie and Maxwellton.

PAISLEY THREAD

Paisley's international pre-eminence in thread manufacture came about in a most curious way. Thread spinning was introduced by Christian Shaw, daughter of the local Laird of Baragan, who, as a young girl, had claimed to have been affected by a servant's curse. Her parents took her to Mr Blackwell, a Paisley minister and infamous 'witch'-hunter, and between them they had six people condemned to death as 'witches' in 1696, strangled and burned at Gallowgreen, and then their ashes buried at a cross roads in George Street. Christian later became a minister's widow and took up spinning thread to eke out her income, using a Dutch device brought home by a relative. Such was her success that the local lairds invested in her business and Lady Esquire, a local noblewoman, was so impressed she spread the word among her English friends at Court. In 1735 Christian's process fortuitously returned to Paisley about the time steam power was coming into use. James Watt was a Greenock man working in Glasgow University when he solved the problem of the working rotary engine.

A steam-powered thread industry rapidly sprang up, and by a series of mergers eventually became a virtual world monopoly dominated by the Coats and the Clarks. Their great industrial conglomerations continued to grow, spawning new tenement suburbs for their key workers and foremen, and new villa suburbs beyond for managers and other administrators and the commercial and industrial entrepreneurs who traded with them.

Improvements in transportation were also taking place. New toll roads were constructed with regular stage coaches to Glasgow and Greenock, and the Glasgow, Paisley and Ardrossan Canal was built as far as Paisley. A new boat building industry grew up in consequence, coming about through the development of lightweight steel boats for the Paisley Canal, fostered by local laird, John Houston. These vessels, each sixty feet long by four feet wide, carried sixty people at a time at 11 mph drawn by two horses. At first the canal bloomed despite a tragedy in 1810 when over one hundred child workers aged twelve to fourteen were drowned when a boat overturned at the quayside in the terminus basin.

Carved floral roundel from now burnt-out school

Largely as a result of these early experiments, Renfrew and Paisley boatyards came to specialise in ferries and dredgers which they supplied throughout the British Empire.

Competition from the railways eventually closed the canal (except for a short length in Coats' thread works used for a water supply), and it was filled in and used as another railway. The railways had come in 1841, first the Glasgow/Wemyss Bay line at Gilmour Street and later the Glasgow/Ardrossan line along the old canal route.

Today the Coats Mills at Ferguslie (Maxwellton) are a dismal sight and site, only the No 1 Spinning Mill (1887) still standing with the ruins of the counting house. A massive, monumental, five-storey cast-iron and concrete building clad in red and yellow brick with gazebo-like corner turrets, the

The geography lesson

mill stands derelict on a desolate rubble-strewn plain. The huge glazed, cast-iron fanlight and canopy of the North Gatehouse (1890), equally abandoned, is nevertheless evocative of the pride of the Victorian Coats in their industry.

The Coats were also caring employers by their rights, rather like present day Japanese companies—from cradle to grave paternalism, they built the Mill dining hall (now a burnt-out shell) as a grand Scots Renaissance building with interesting carved detail and the Ferguslie School (now a night-club) to encourage education in their workers, and the Girls' Club & Hostel for single women. The school, known formerly as the 'Half-Timers School', is a monument to the Coats, the 'Medicis' of Victorian Paisley rather than a simple functional building such as that at New Lanark. It has wonderful white marble carvings celebrating learning and geography and a polished granite portico reminiscent of a Florentine loggia. The red sandstone club and hostel is also beautifully detailed with Glasgow style dreaming girls' heads carved over the doors.

The Coats looked after their workers, providing housing in the vicinity of George Street, Queen Street and Argyle Street while across the canal lay the grander Castlehead, a leafy suburb of Victorian houses engulfing, at No.14 Main Road, an existing black-and-white Georgian farmhouse.

At the other end of George Street, across the Cart, lay the Anchor Mills complex of Robert Clark with its associated housing at Williamsburgh and villas at Greenlaw and Ralston. Rather more of this mill complex has survived but isolated now across an extended Eastend Park created by the

The vast interior of the Ferguslie spinning mill

cavalier destruction of the town centre in favour of the new county headquarters and the earlier cleaning up of the tightly built-up Abbey Close by the conservation and restoration movement.

Most of the mills were designed by the Bradford firm of Woodhouse & Morley and the actual Anchor Mills with its Pompidou like external stairs and wonderful cast-iron atrium, surely is a deserving monument for which a proper use must be found if it is to be conserved for posterity.

In Kilnside Road we can see not only the magnificent Mile End Mill, with its monumental chimney and decorative cupola, but also the social stratification of the community, the foremen in the bay windowed tenements at the top of the hill, the ordinary workers in the simpler tenements at the foot of the hill nearest the mill.

THE TENEMENT TOWN

The Bull Inn in New Street

Some relief from the austerity of these stone cliffs is given by the vigorous and colourful bars and the local 'wee shops'. Paisley is a place for connoisseurs of bars, with its Edwardian-fantasy Burgh Bar, Lacy Street; Harvie's Bar, Glasgow Road; the 'new Victorian' Corkers in Causeyside Street; and the old Wee Howf, in the High Street. Also in Causeyside Street is the Tea Garden Tavern, 'a great name for a pub' as well as Faither's.

These public houses enliven their streets in a vigorous and decorative way. The finest of them undoubtedly is the Glasgow style Bull Inn is 7 New Street, designed in 1900-1 by William (Willie) McLennan (1872-1940), a local self-trained architect. Like all his work, the Bull Inn is intriguingly detailed, beautifully lit and very practically planned. The tenement, of which the bar is the ground floor, has a curious Arthur Rackham quality, characteristic of McLennan, whose lack of formal training subtly shows from time to time. This particular tenement was built for Charles Stevenson, a wine and spirit merchant, but the tenement is a building type often built for speculation.

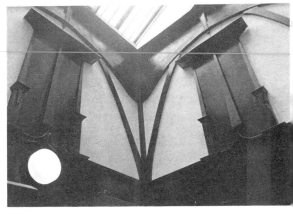

The atrium of the Bull Inn

At the end of the nineteenth-century the wealth created by the thread and textile industry, and its burgeoning industrial infrastructure, found outlet in speculation in the building of residential and office tenements and retailing enterprises along the town streets. High-density building and rebuilding took place leaving – amusingly, in some cases – a one or two-storey vernacular building squashed between massive tenement 'bookends'.

Speculation and need determined this widespread tenement building but the illusion that the Scottish tenement is a dull and monotonous building style is soon dispelled by the astonishing variety to found in Paisley. It is often forgotten that in

Scotland, and in Europe generally, the tenement is the home of all classes and not as our English neighbours seem to think, a building reserved only for the poor.

An 'inhabited wall' the tenement defines and is defined by the street; it often displays a proliferation of skillful detailing, interesting elevations and vying styles often relating to the social class of the occupants, like for example the tower at the corner of Neilston Road and Stock Street or the 'baronial' tenements at Carriagehill Drive and Brodie Park Avenue. Paisley's main streets have much to offer an architectural browser.

SUBURBS

The erection of stately, middle-class tenements and handsome terraced streets was followed by the development of 'garden' suburbs which spread out, along and up the valley of the Cart. These villas and bungalows have their own astonishing variety from straight 'Victorian' classical to the quirky Glasgow style of W D McLennan, who built at least three fascinating villas at Nos 10, 12 and 31 Thornley Park Avenue.

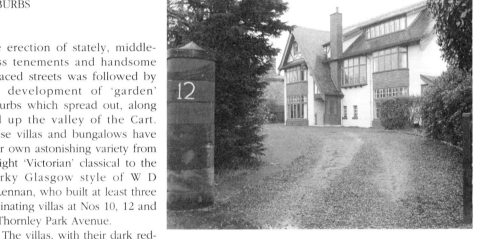

McLennan Villa at 12 Thornly Park Avenue

The villas, with their dark red-painted half-timbering, cream rendering and green Welsh slates, might be described as being closer to Voysey rather than to Mackintosh. The interiors are wonderfully spacious with tall, well-lit halls, usually lit through a stained-glass window giving a warm coloured light from the north, allowing all the main rooms to face the sun.

Ardyne, built in 1910, is the nearest to Mackintosh; with a hall reminiscent of Windyhill, but with a great range of horizontal windows on the front, heavily modelled in bays. The porch is spectacular, being disturbingly cantilevered. Glenarm is the most exciting inside with a huge square hall wrapped round by a stair and gallery and a wonderful inglenook fireplace under the stair.

Later on in 1924-6 he built a most interesting concrete house at Thorscrag on the Barrhead Road, reinforced concrete walls and floors, a precast red sandstone exterior with the most extraordinary detailing. This is one of the most unusual houses in Scotland. Don't miss the enormous cantilevered chimney copes which are a clue to the peculiarity of its construction.

Yet another interesting group of garden-city houses was built at Potterhill for Brown & Polson's employees. These seeming semi-detached houses, in the manner of Unwin & Parker of Welwyn Gardon City fame, when examined more closely, turn out to be Scottish flatted blocks, virtually tenements disguised as semi-detached houses, a bit of an architectural *tour de force*.

Incidentally Brown & Polsons patent Cornflour was a clever bye-product of the linen industry being produced by a patent process from the starch manufactured for the linen industry.

Paisley is a place where all is not always what it seems. The famous golliwog of Golden Shred Marmalade, another Paisley product, comes from the weavers' dissenting interest in slave emancipation, and a visit to Paisley by Harriet Beecher Stowe, the great American emancipator. During the fund-raising tour of her famous play Uncle Tom's Cabin, Paisley children were excited and impressed and made negro dolls from old black stockings, giving them, as children will, nonsense names, one of which adhered and was selected as the famous trademark, now viewed by some as an object of racial discrimination but then seen as a badge of sympathy.

TOWN CENTRE

Commercial developments and public buildings kept pace with the tenement and villa construction. The Clark town hall with its classic façade offset by curious asymmetrical towers, had a carillon which played a medley of Scottish traditional airs and stands across the road from the Methodist central halls which have great oversized urns on the façade.

The late nineteenth-century was a period of development in retailing, and the two famous Paisley-based Cochrane's and Galbraith's grocery chain stores flourished and spread to Glasgow and the rest of the west of Scotland at this time.

Paisley's Clark Town Hall

HIGH STREET

The original burghal buildings of the seventeenth-century were unhesitatingly demolished in the High Street, and the Georgian buildings, too, to allow the creation at pavement level of a wall of the recently invented plate glass. These wide-fronted shops were topped by commercial offices for let, the whole having a splendid scale and vigour.

Looking more closely, adjacent to the cross we have a splendid scholarly classical piece from John Honeyman, who was Charles Rennie Mackintosh's hero and employer. What a pity, though, he did not seek to incorporate the historic tolbooth which previously stood here.

Next comes a series of repetitive but subtly varied office blocks with shops below. Built about 1880 these have the traditional classical parti of base, piano nobile and attic stories but re-interpreted with Victorian vigour, all interesting variations on an architectural theme.

Modern High Street shop fronts

I have strong reservations when confronting the recent example where a cavalier contemporary hand has swept away the original bottom floor replacing it with a banal modelled glass front. One day, nevertheless, it might be seen as an example of twentieth-century innovation.

On the south side of the street, the ubiquitous contemporary chain stores obliterate any character of place in favour of their corporate, i.e. private, image for private gain, and ignore the laudable contributions of their Victorian predecessors across the way. Paisley has been singularly unfortunate in this respect.

Along at the start of the old meal market from which New Street descends, is an attractive functional 'Moderne' commercial building of the 1930s with a rather dull Victorian YMCA beyond. Smaller surviving burgh houses follow, giving an impression of the scale of the early burgh. A look back at the High Street from nearby Weighbridge Close reveals the turnpike stairs at the back of these original houses.

Across the High Street at Orr Square, a curiously non-existent square this, is a splendid little black and chrome *art deco* corner, delightfully typical of the 1930s, and a two-storey shop, Clare's Furs, with some stylish lettering in a similar style which is possibly 1980s revival.

WEST END AND CAUSEYSIDE

*Steel
Maitlands'
Russell
Institute*

Victorian architects were acutely conscious of the singularity of the 'corner', as a look around at Paisley's varied turrets will reveal. The gushet tenement at Westend Cross presents a striking architectural build up, with a pyramidal roof, a clock tower and interesting cast-iron shop-fronts along its frontages. Going south down St Mirin and Causeyside streets, the skill and ambitions of the tenement architects can be seen in great variety. Turreted corners abound, and architectural styles, baronial and Glasgow style, tease more sober beaux-arts intruders, but everywhere can be found a display of architectural skill in the service of enlightened patronage.

The Victorian and Edwardian client understood his private responsibility in the public domain, happily paying for sculpture and decent materials while his architect understood the ordering of both social hierarchy and that of place and the need to 'landmark' the town, making it comprehensible.

The huge Edwardian Co-operative Offices are a splendid monument to working-class ambition, a reminder of artisan pride in the job and the stubborn independence engendered by the weaving ethos.

Steel Maitland's Russell Institute (1926-7), with its stylised sculptures by Archibald Dawson, is a fitting building of a younger era, together with the older Peddie & Kinnear baronial tenement across the way, which also has a bevelled and accentuated corner, makes a fine pair of gateposts to the town centre approached from the south.

The left hand one is a vigorous example of Glasgow style tinged with baronial; the other, by contrast, is more geometric and abstract. It incorporates a memorial to David Stow (1793,1864), another 'Paisley buddie' who was a figure of national importance. He was the Victorian educator who established the first teacher training college in Britain, the 'Normal School' in Glasgow, in 1836, and influenced teaching throughout Britain. This memorial is a further reminder of the value the weavers placed on education, and of how examination of an environment reveals the character of the community who built it.

At the gushet of Causeyside and Neilston and Cartside Roads is a bizarre 'signpost' tower spectacularly rising at least twenty feet above the roof. Down to the left is a fine little Glasgow style building, now not unsuitably used as a night club.

*Sculptures of
sick children
on Russell
Institute
BOTTOM:
The
sculpture
crowning the
Russell
Institute*

In Gordon Street, just off Causeyside, is an interesting and unusual city block now isolated as a traffic island. One end is the Victorian Central Fire Station with a Scottish conical-capped turret, and an absurd Italian gothic hose tower, an import in miniature from San Gimingiano.

At the other end of the block, fronting the abyss of the ring road roundabouts, is W. D. McLennan's St Matthew's Church (1905-7). This church is a more eccentric art nouveau building than Mackintosh's earlier Queen's Cross Church (1896-9), Garscube Road, Glasgow. The belfry spire, which was never built, had exaggerated, tulip-like version of the Scottish crown steeple seen to such effect at the Coats Memorial Church. The inside is quirky rather than elegant, the stained glass patterns odd rather than mythic, and the trusses outre, more like continental art nouveau. It is beautifully lit and McLennan's practicality shows in the rigorous planning of the sanctuary and choir arrangements, and in the unusual rake in the floor, to cope with the length of the nave.

MODERN (E) PAISLEY

But William McLennan is not the only interesting architect to have been born in Paisley. Later in the century Paisley acquired a particularly fine set of 'Moderne' buildings by another native son, Thomas Tait (1882-1954), of Burnet Tait & Lorne in London.

Hawkhead Hospital–though much altered since its erection in the mid-1930s–is one of the best examples of this genre anywhere in Britain. Formerly specialising in infectious diseases, this hospital effortlessly expresses the confidence in hygiene and health of the Modern movement in a way that makes the feeble Post modern offering of the Volvo Showroom on Glasgow Road seem as trivial as it is.

Hawkhead Hospital

The hospital buildings not only seek to exploit sunlight and fresh air but to gain some pleasure out of it. Look at these adventurous cantilevered hoods over the balconies and the coloured tiles, cheerful and decorative, which were meant to be enjoyed. Look, too, at the sheer stylishness of the long, low, liner-like lines.

Tait must have been extremely pleased to have landed such an important commission in his home town. Success bred success: later, in 1936, he won the most important competition of the decade, for St Andrew's House in Edinburgh, home of the Scottish Office, and in 1938 went on to design the Empire Exhibition, in particular the spectacular Symbolic Tower that bore his name, 'Tait's Tower'.

Otherwise the later twentieth-century is mostly depressingly insensitive. The system built county buildings look what they are, a

mechanistic solution to a bureaucratic problem uninterested in the onlookers point of view. Let us hope they will soon be decently hidden behind the trees. A bank across the road by the same architects reveals how they would have allowed this 'system' to creep like some alien growth over the whole town till it was totally absorbed by its amorphous mass creating a faceless mini 'metropolis' full of appropriate workers.

It almost makes you grateful for post modern. Trivial though it usually is it does make an effort to charm, as the examples of the Kelburn Cinema and the Glasgow Road Volvo Showroom, show.

'Upton' - thought to be by Basil Spence

PAISLEY

The burgh of Paisley was a real set of surprises. The ancient abbey turned out to be mostly fake, invented by Victorian and Edwardian restorers, but the apparently monotonous nineteenth-century tenement town was really quite complex and far from dull and there were some splendid moments in the twentieth-century suburbs.

We learned the character of a community could be read in the kind and quality of building they choose to embellish their town, and we discovered two intriguing architects, one quirky, the other mainstream, but both Paisley buddies.

We saw that the ancient street lines and property boundaries persisted despite later rebuilding and the ravages of the traffic engineers, letting us determine the size and shape of the original burgh, and see the classic stages of growth: first the Georgian infill, then a new town, or in Paisley's case new towns, beyond the original limits, and then the Victorian expansion in the wake of its burgeoning textile industry followed by the massive sprawl engendered by the motor car.

I hope that Paisley showed us that even the most apparently prosaic place can offer a worthwhile adventure of discovery, given the effort to look.

V

STIRLING

Bruce, Bannockburn and the Blenheim Bomber

Perched on a great stone outcrop overlooking what was the lowest bridging point on the River Forth, Stirling commands the gateway to the Highlands. Throughout its independent history it has been at the centre of Scotland's struggle against its warlike neighbour, England, and of its own fratricidal strife. At least four historic battle sites are visible from Stirling on a good day.

Across the valley on another rocky prominence can be seen the monument to Sir William Wallace, the lowly lowland laird who roused Scotland to a sense of nationhood, winning the Battle of Stirling Bridge in 1297 and going on to become her guardian before his tragic betrayal and untimely death. Further down the valley is the Field of Bannockburn where, in 1314, Scotland's supreme hero and warrior king, Robert Bruce confirmed that nationhood in a mighty victory that 'sent Proud Edward homewards to think again', and established for once and all, the powerful commitment to freedom which has come to characterise the Scottish people.

Where better to begin to look at what a burgh was and is than in this most royal of Scottish burghs, which still possesses its charter, its walls and traces of its gates,

The Tolbooth

its tolbooth and its mercat cross, a high school and a High Kirk where John Knox preached and King James VI & I was christened, not to mention a castle in whose chapel Mary Queen of Scots was married. It even still has a dungeon, now dramatically embedded within a new shopping centre, a symbol perhaps of Scotland's past and present.

Broad Street, in the very heart of the burgh, is the old mercat or market place where trading took place twice-weekly. In the Middle Ages there were no shops as we know them now, and the right to hold a market for buying and selling and the right to ban all other trading and manufacture locally was a vital economic privilege. The mercat cross was the visible evidence of that right and also the place of proclamation, and of the striking of bargains. In Stirling the unicorn or 'puggy', as it is known locally, on the top of the cross is not only itself a royal beast but it sports the royal lion of Scotland on the shield it bears proclaiming royal assent to the market. The puggy is original but the shaft-supporting steps are replacements, erected in 1891, the first cross having been removed in 1792, an early 'traffic improvement'.

Beyond the cross is the tolbooth, or town house, a stately manifestation of the burgh's right to self-government. Here the town council met and deliberated, tolls were fixed, malcontents gaoled, and the burgh's revenues and weapons securely stored. An excellent example of the early Renaissance, its tower, topped with a little ogee-roofed pavilion was designed by Sir William Bruce, the architect of the Palace of Holyroodhouse, to whom the town's mason, Harry Livingston, was sent 'to obtain a scheme', a sign surely of high ambition on the part of Stirling's burgesses. It has a clock, which until 1940 played a medley of Scots tunes on the hour. The west or mercat front was extended a further three bays by Gideon Gray, a local architect, in 1785. At the rear, a late extension built to house the new court house and gaol, has simple classical lines, set off by a vigorous sculpted doorway. Designed in 1806 by Richard Crichton, the council thought the fees then were too high and invited two cut-price architects to finish the job, something not unknown to today's developers (and architects).

The Doorway of the Tolbooth's 1906 extension

Directly across the market is a good example of a typical seventeenth-century (1671) burgher's house. Built for James Norie, the then town clerk, its vertical gabled form clearly derives, as do those of many similar burghal houses from Dutch or Flemish houses in the ports with which the burgh traded. Norie's son became town clerk in his turn, a typical example of the nepotism rife in burghal society. Conversion to housing in the

1950s has bowdlerised the ground floor, which formerly featured a shop, its removal contributing to the rather dead feeling nowadays in what was once the burgh's busiest and most lively space; a defect Stirling should address in these days of tourist Scotland. The house features interesting diamond-faceted columns and pedimented windows with Latin inscriptions above 'A Good Conscience is a Brazen Wall' is one particularly appropriate for a town clerk.

Norie's House

At the foot of the market place another burgh house can be found: 'Darnley's House', so-called because Mary Queen of Scots' consort is reputed to have preferred to lodge here rather than in the castle when they were together in Stirling; actually, he stayed in a tavern, Willie Bell's, behind the house. Erskine of Gogar was the owner and builder of this town house, dating from the sixteenth and seventeenth-centuries. Traces of its former appearance remain in the arcaded ground floor and the dormers, the curved one of which, albeit rather untypical, nevertheless was emulated at Fochabers by a local turn-of-the-century architect, James MacLaren, from whom in turn it was copied by Charles Rennie Mackintosh in a house he designed in Comrie.

Typically in a Scottish burgh, the narrow burgage plots or tofts behind the street houses were developed as the town grew, and to the rear of 'Darnley's House' we find, entering through the pend, yet another seventeenth-century house. It was owned originally by Moir of Leckie, and then by the Stirlings of Keir, who added fine Palladian windows in the eighteenth-century to afford them a view of their country seat across the valley.

Darnley's House at the foot of Broad Street

What a shame the town falls apart at this point, thanks to the misguided zeal of the sanitisers of the 1950s. There is some hope today, however, that the pressure of tourism and growing interest in museums and archaeology might generate some radical reconstruction of the centre if the bureaucracy of building control can allow intelligence the chance to operate.

Mar's Wark

Turning our backs on 'Darnley's House' and looking up the hill we see dominating the market – as its builder once dominated Scotland – Mar's Wark, the splendid ruins of a sixteenth-century palace, home of a great Renaissance nobleman, and Regent of Scotland: the Earl of Mar. Damaged

in 1746 in an attack on the castle during the last Jacobite uprising it remains an imposing terminal to the principal public space of the burgh. The wark was built in 1570-2 by Lord Erskine, hereditary governor of Stirling Castle, to celebrate his elevation to the Earldom of Mar on becoming guardian to Mary Queen of Scots' baby son, the future King James VI & I. It has the usual Renaissance parti or layout, the accommodation is arranged around a gated courtyard with the guard room, stores, kitchens etc on the ground floor, and the piano nobile or principal accommodation, the hall and reception rooms at first floor which has lofty ceilings and big fireplaces, making it a fitting place to receive and entertain in the style expected of the nobility. The rude but vigorous carved external embellishment is in the Scottish tradition, copy-book Renaissance details with

*A stai
tower c
Mar's War*

a sprinkling of pious admonitions and heraldry thrown in. The two symmetrical towers flanking the gateway contained the stairs. The coats of arms of both the Earl and the Monarch are displayed over the entrance, and the mermaids on the soffit of the balconies inform us on the one hand who it was built for, and under whose auspices, and on the other that the outside, at least, was meant for public enjoyment and wonder.

Downhill to the left we see the rounded apse of the Church of the Holy Rude or the High Kirk, another essential burghal attribute to which we shall return. Beyond it in Spittal Street are more typical burgh houses. The very Scottish turnpike stair identifies that of a local laird, Bruce of Auchenbowie; built about 1520, it has a vaulted basement, a curious double crow-stepped gable and a finely ornamented door.

Across the road is a boys' club, a 1929 reconstruction in a jokey baronial style, beloved in cultivated Edinburgh circles, with slightly comic mottoes addressed to the boys– the Scouts and the Boys Brigade–for whom the club was built: 'Play the Game', 'Keep Smiling', and, my own favourite, 'Quarrelling is Taboo'.

Motto on Boys' Club

These inscriptions may make you smile, but they identify contemporary social attitudes and Stirling is strong on pawky mottoes as will be seen later.

Further down Spittal Street at a point where there used be a burn, a small group of buildings is all that remains of the former continuously built-up 'street wall'. These are Darrow's Ludging and Spittal's Hospital. A ludging was where a local nobleman or laird – in this case Sir James Darrow— would lodge when in town, but would also exploit as a property for rent .

Erected in the sixteenth-century (1521), Darrow's Ludging was renovated with ghastly good taste around 1937. Typically harled with dressed stone margins round the doors and windows, it features another turnpike stair and some unusual 'gothic' windows, allegedly relating to a period when it was used as an Episcopalian chapel, but much more likely to be a fashionable whimsy of the gothic Revival.

Its 'hospital' neighbour dates from the seventeenth-century, but has been much altered, first in Victorian times and again more recently in 1959 when its turret stair was rebuilt. On the front is an interesting carved panel, a genuine commemorative store which features tailors' scissors and the inscription:

> This house is foundit for the support of the puir
> be Robert Spittall tailyour to King James, the 4 in
> anno 1530

This stone was probably removed from Spittal's original hospital when it was demolished in 1751 and placed here in this other house owned by the hospital which, over the years, had acquired much property in and around Stirling. The panel acts as a reminder of the role the merchants and tradesmen played in looking after the poor and infirm of the burgh and it is interesting to observe that Heriot's Hospital in Edinburgh was built by James VI's goldsmith, while Spittal's here in Stirling was gifted by his tailor; clearly, James was a well-dressed, well-heeled king.

COWANE'S HOSPITAL

Another larger hospital can be found at the top of the hill next to the Church of the Holy Rude, donated this time by James Cowane, a seventeenth-century Dean of Guild and Provost who lived in a fine house in St Mary's Wynd next to the north gate. The commemoration stone informs us he left 40,000 merks in 1633 for the succour of twelve decayed gildbreither, and in 1639 John Mylne (of Inverary fame) was appointed architect. Later, in 1852, it was converted to a splendid guild-hall by the removal of a floor and the insertion of fine large windows overlooking the carse.

E-shaped in plan with a central tower and crow-stepped gables, the hospital is once again harled with stone dressings. The founder's statue gazes down from a niche above the door. There is a local rumour that old 'Staneybreeks', as he is familiarly known, used to come to life every 'Ne'er'day' and join in the festivities, his absence lately being explained by failure to hear the bells owing to deafness in his old age. A pair of fine decorative lamp-posts flank the entrance, a reminder of Cowane's provostship, no doubt.

Old
Staneybreeks

The adjacent bowling green dates back to 1712 and the cannon on the terrace were made nearby at the Carron Iron Works, sold to Russia which used them against us in the Bosphorus; captured in 1855 at Sebastapol they were brought back home to grace the green–whether as monuments to victory or folly is open to choice.

CEMETERY

Between the Guild Hall and the church, steps lead up to the cemetery where many headstones of burgesses can be found. Beautifully carved and decorated with guild marks, and symbols of trade and death, they are well worth a browse. Fine views of the more important buildings of the burgh can be obtained from the cemetery. The castle, the High Kirk, the old high school, and Argyll's Ludging all abutt on or are adjacent to the graveyard.

Stirling's cemetery is one of its great pleasures, a treasure-trove of finely carved stones and interesting memorials. In the Middle Ages the Valley Graveyard, as it is now known, was probably a medieval tilt yard and the Ladies Rock, the little eminence in the middle, reputedly was a vantage-point from which the ladies of the court could watch the knights

The Castle from the Ladies Rock

exercise and joust. Later it became an extension to the kirkyard when outdoor burial became popular.

Gravestones on the whole were, and are, expensive and thus a sure sign of status, particularly in the past, so a visit to a graveyard is always enlightening, and changing attitudes to death and to people are clearly visible. For instance, on the whole, former clergy are of little interest to us now, but as their columns and obelisks here show, in the nineteenth century congregations clearly vied with each other in the splendour of their minister's monuments, much as Italian cities used to compete in building higher and higher towers to express their civic pride.

In the beginning, important people–landowners, provosts, bailies and the like–were buried or commemorated inside the church to such an extent that whole aisles and chapels were devoted to single families.

In the sixteenth and seventeenth centuries burial outside in the ground became

*The
Graveyard*

common and the first external tombs followed the old pattern of flat carved slabs; later they were capped to throw off the rain; later still raised on legs (table tombs); and finally upright headstones became common. Interestingly, such gravestones occur much earlier in Scotland than in England and some splendid examples can be found around the guild-hall and Kirk of the Holy Rude.

Two other monuments of particular interest are the Star Pyramid, a large granite pyramid honouring the covenanting dead; and the Martyrs' Monument, a fine little glass cupola with sculptured figures inside, commemorating Margaret Wilson and Margaret McLachlan, two Presbyterian women, one little more than a girl, who were tied to stakes and drowned on the sands at Wigton in 1685 for their faith. Both monuments were erected in 1858 by William Drummond, a local worthy of considerable religious fanaticism who made his fortune with the publication of Sunday tracts, immensely popular Victorian religious reading.

CHURCH OF THE HOLY RUDE

From the graveyard looking back, a fine view is obtained of the Church of the Holy Rude, with its complex eighty-five foot high tower. This is Stirling's High Kirk which originally stood clear at the top of the town, nearer to God, and the nobles, far above the poor and the stench of the shambles, cesspits and tanneries below. Cruciform in plan, dating from about 1450, it is an important building in the town and in history. Here in 1567 John Knox preached on the occasion of the Protestant crowning of Mary Queen of Scots. Here, too, was christened the son of Mary and Lord Darnley, the prince who became James VI of Scotland and James I of England.

*The Church
of the Holy
Rude*

Dating from 1456 to 1470, the church retains its tower and the nave with its vaulted aisles and original medieval timber roof somewhat mutilated by James Gillespie Graham, a Victorian 'improver' who built up the West door and removed many of the guild chapels. Massive central piers indicate the founder's intention to build a spire at the crossing.

The nave with its curious cusped windows is horizontal in emphasis, but the later choir, the inner space reserved for the clergy, is vertical in its effect. Begun in 1507 in the realm of James IV, the choir took another fifty years to complete. The building of the church was financed by Dunfermline Abbey where Charles I was born, and by the income from fines from the Court of the Four Burghs. In 1656, after one of those disputes for which Scottish churches are famous, a wall was built to separate the choir and nave, and the building contained two churches until 1936 when the factions were reconciled (or running costs were getting too high) and James Miller removed the wall and modified the pillars.

Among its many interesting features inside are the whiskered crowned head and figure opposite with stuck-out tongue on either side of the chancel and, outside, the carved rose and thistle marking James IV's chapel built to commemorate his marriage to Margaret Tudor. The church clock dates from 1519 and the font and inscribed panels in the tower are also worthy of note, the latter commemorating and praising the benefactors of the church. Inside, too, the power of the burgesses can be seen in their burial lairs in the aisles and in the two remaining private commemorative chapels, which were created by knocking out a window and extending the church outwards (St Andrew's chapel 1483, St Mary's chapel 1484).

Originally called the Parish Church of Stirling, it was renamed the Parish Church of Holy Cross in 1525 and in 1545 was raised to collegiate status justifying six priests and a musician. After the Reformation in 1560 it became a Protestant church and, around 1590, renamed the Rude Church of Stirling. The kirk's role in the burgh was to provide a locus for collective worship, to aid the poor, to encourage education and to persecute 'unbelievers'. In 1621 a certain John Smyth was fined for wandering through the fields unnecessarily at the time of the sermon, an example of the activities of the elders or the 'unco guid', as Burns dubbed them.

Argyll's Ludging from the Churchyard

ARGYLL'S LUDGING

From behind Mar's wark in the churchyard another attractive, interesting view is to be had of Scotland's finest surviving nobleman's mansion, the oldest part built in the sixthteenth-century for Lord Alexander of Tullibody, a poet and a favourite of Charles I who made him Earl of Stirling and Viscount of Canada. This building later passed into the hands of the 9th Earl of Argyll who extended it to its present size about 1674. He and his

One of the stair towers– Argyll's Ludging

retinue lodged there when in attendance at the Court. Entered through a magnificent rusticated stone gateway in the harled screen wall of the courtyard it presents a symmetrical façade with a pedimented Doric porch in the centre, an armorial cartouche above and four stair towers capped by conical roofs which give it a strong baronial presence. This is a good example of early Scottish Renaissance, vernacular building made symmetrical, with fashionable Flemish cartouches around the windows. Inside it has interesting fireplaces and a painted ceiling and panelling in the upper hall, appropriate to a great nobleman's mansion. In its day it has been a nobleman's lodging, a military hospital and a youth hostel.

The cartouche– Argyll's Ludging

HIGH SCHOOL

Across the way from the Argyll Ludging, lying below the esplanade is the pedimented high school built in 1788 by Gideon Gray. This building, now a hotel, incorporates some of the stonework of the earlier fifteenth-century grammar school which took over from the monastic school after the Reformation. Gideon Gray was the first professional architect to live in Stirling, and was a freeman of the burgh in 1769. He was also responsible for the extension to the front of the tolbooth and for Wingate's Inn, now the Golden Lion Hotel.

From the castle esplanade above, a splendid view obtains over the Forth towards the Wallace Monument of 1861-9 by J. J. Rochead and the University of Stirling, completed 1967 onwards, Robert Matthew, Johnson-Marshall & Partners, a group of interesting modern buildings in a wooded parkland setting which are well worth a visit.

Appropriately, on the esplanade a visitors' centre (1971) has been created in an old hotel formerly entered from Upper Castlehill Street below. Designed by Edinburgh architects, Edwin Johnson and Nicholas Groves-Raines, it demonstrates creative re-use of an older building, with some stimulating twentieth-century innovations.

Particularly exciting are the cantilevered 'Blenheim Nose Cone' windows where if you have a good head for heights you can step out into space and look out over the view or back at the building. I doubt if the architects knew the Blenheim Bomber, the Bulldog Fighter of First World War fame and the Beaufort Fighter of the Second, were designed by a Stirling man called Frank Branwell who, with his brothers, built and flew their first plane in 1909.

At their instigation the first air race in Britain, for the enormous prize then of £10,000, was from London to Stirling and back. The planes flew up the east coast landed in the King's Park beside the King's Knot and then flew down the west coast.

Inside the centre, apart from the serried ranks of fudge and tartan souvenirs, a splendidly sculpted little audio-visual auditorium provides an opportunity to view a historical presentation before going out to see the real objects all around.

STIRLING CASTLE

At the end of the esplanade, lies Stirling's primary reason for existence: the castle. Securely walled above high bleak crags the castle sits 250 feet high on the leading edge of a whale-backed volcanic rocky outcrop. Below it, along the ridge, the burgh gently descends to the valley bottom in a fashion not dissimilar to Edinburgh. This rock has probably been fortified since prehistoric times, certainly Roman coins have been found on it. By the medieval era it had become a residence of the Canmore Dynasty of Kings of Scotland. It was a frequent prize in the struggle between Scotland and England, most significantly when its promised surrender became the particular cause of the Battle of Bannockburn. Later it was a favourite haunt of the Stewart kings.

Stirling Castle from Bannockburn

In its present condition it demonstrates a continuity of military development over many centuries since the first stone walls were erected at the beginning of the thirteenth-century. The outer defences were built by Queen Anne early in the eighteenth-century and were designed for defence against artillery and rifle fire. Entrance is across a drawbridge over a ditch running along the length of battlemented wall with corbelled ogee, turreted sentry boxes, and a projecting 'French spur' battery to provide covering fire for the bridge and gate.

The esplanade is a late parade ground built on what was the clear open space left as a 'killing ground' between the castle and the town.

The New Port (or new gateway) is a simple rusticated doorway leading through the outer defences into a small courtyard, Guardroom Square, protected by a covered battery (Queen Anne Battery) under which access is gained to the

sixteenth-century forework–everybody's idea of what a castle entrance should look like. Slezer's seventeenth-century print gives some idea of how it must have looked in former times

Built in the reign of James IV, the four flanking turrets of which two remain were formerly a storey higher and capped by conical roofs like a fairytale castle, till Cromwell's General Monk reduced them in 1651. The gateway still retains its original vaulted entrance and a portcullis. At each end of the forework wall stand fortified towers, the Prince's Tower to the west and the Elphinstone to the east.

James V's Renaissance Palace

The foundations of the two demolished towers at the base of the wall can still be seen.

Beyond the gateway, inside the original keep, lies the Lower Square, an impressive space flanked by the splendid frenchified façade of James V's Renaissance Palace (1540) and, facing ahead, the gable of the Cochrane's medieval Great Hall, constructed or reconstructed in the same period as the forework. These two buildings are considered the finest examples of the architecture of the period in Scotland. The smaller buildings on the right are the kitchens and the north port and nether bailey, the old gateway to the Highlands.

The Great Hall

Under a connecting covered bridge, up a steep slope between the palace and the hall, the road rises to give access to the Upper Square. This in turn is contained by the palace, the King's Old Buildings and the Chapel Royal rebuilt in the 1550s by Jame VI. To the south it is bounded by the medieval entrance façade of the Great Hall. More of a set piece in its way, and better than anything Edinburgh Castle has to offer, this square still conveys something of the atmosphere of the great days of the castle.

The guid man O' Ballengeich

The palace itself is a three-storey, quadrangular building arranged around a central court known as the 'Lions' Den' where the palace zoo was reputedly sited. This is the grandest early Renaissance building in Scotland, with its royal suites in the grand piano nobile, over a lower floor of vaulted cellars which takes up the fall in the site and up above an attic of servants' lodgings squeezed inside the roof, revealed now by a somewhat crude nineteenth-century window inserted through the cornice.

The heavily modelled outer façades are orderly and symmetrical - instantly recognisable Renaissance characteristics - and are ornamented with carvings, niches and statues ranging from the serene to the comic, 'All human life' is there (as the *News of the World* used to boast), including a statue of James himself in Highland dress, a reference to his habit of circulating in disguise as the 'guid man of Ballengeich'. His French Queen, Mary of Guise, is reputed to have brought over with her the French masons whose handiwork is clear in these highly decorative façades.

Now entered through a modest porch in the north-west corner, the king's and the queens' suites of apartments are arranged round three sides of the court (the fourth fell down in the seventeenth-century. The king's is on the left, comprising respectively the King's Guard Hall, the Royal Presence Chamber and the Royal Bed Chamber. A similar arrangement for the queen is reached off a western gallery but their bed chambers conveniently adjoined. Some idea of their former grandeur can be judged by the scale of the remaining fireplaces, and the remnants of the Stirling Heads, powerfully carved portraits of the king and his nobles which now adorn the walls but once formed a highly decorative ceiling in the king's apartments in the palace.

Adjoining the palace is the King's Old Building, re-built after a fire in 1857, reputed to contain the room where James II murdered the Earl of Douglas in 1452 and had his body tossed out the window. It has recently been adapted to provide a regimental museum and headquarters for the Argyll & Sutherland Highlanders and is largely visited for its contents rather than its architecture.

CHAPEL ROYAL

At least the second royal chapel on this site, a chapel certainly is mentioned in the earliest reference to the castle in 1124. What we see now is a Renaissance re-building in 1594 for the christening of Prince Henry, James VI's heir. The king had to pay a heavy bonus to the masons to ensure its completion on time, suggesting there is nothing new in the building game. Its Renaissance origin is again revealed by its symmetrical appearance with three pairs of arched windows to each side of a splendid central doorway

The Chapel Royal

designed very much *a la mode* to resemble a triumphal arch. In 1628 the ceiling and walls were decorated with murals by a painter called Valentin Jenkin.

In the peace following the Union of the Crowns this building was much debased and converted to barracks accommodation but the removal of inserted floors in the 1930s revealed fragments of these fine paintings and exposed the original form of the chapel.

GREAT HALL (or Parliament House)

On the lower side the Upper Square lies the Great Hall, started possibly by James III's favourite architect, James Cochrane, but completed in its present form by James IV in the early 1500s.

External it seems a very simple building with a row of high-level windows which reveal the massive structure of the wall and a great projecting bay window. The original porch is gone, partly as a result of raising the ground level to create underground water-storage cisterns, but drawings on display inside give an idea of what it may have looked like, and the corbels which once supported it can still be seen. Entered originally through a porch at the north end of the west wall, the 126 foot by 37 foot hall had a royal dais and private entrance from the palace at the other end. A minstrels' gallery above the screened entrance vestibule and a side gallery made the simple hall much more complex than at first sight. The inside of the projecting oriel windows is decoratively vaulted and vast, while huge open fireplaces decorated with simple columns heat the hall on both sides. Since the army left the castle in 1964 investigations and speculations have led to an ongoing reconstruction programme intended to reinstate the Great Hall to its medieval splendour.

The Assembly Rooms from the Municipal Building

GEORGIAN STIRLING

When the palace economy ceased to be important in Stirling the focus of the town moved downhill to the main thoroughfare and in particular to King Street, the medieval meal market which now became the focus of the town's economic and social life. The town gates were demolished to open it up (their trace can still be seen in the street setts). The insalubrious shambles and tanneries and the old run-down, narrow-front, timber and medieval thatched houses were removed to be replaced by genteel wide-front Georgian houses built in finely dressed ashlar stone, with tall, elegant sash windows and slated roofs. These can still be seen lining King Street, albeit coarsened now by unsympathetic twentieth-century shopfronts.

It was here in the new town centre that the Georgians erected their contemporary equivalent of the tolbooth, not a council chamber for a privileged few but an assembly room where local society from the town and round about could meet and socialise. Built in 1816, the year after Waterloo and five centuries after Bannockburn, the Atheneum still stands proudly at the top of King Street, a refined monument to Georgian values, a symbol of settled times and civilised ways. Its elegant, curved façade is dignified by a tall Renaissance tower topped by a fine steeple, like some London church, almost but not quite spoiled by a proto pop-art porch with an outsized Wallace on top, added in 1859.

On the right is the Golden Lion Hotel or Wingate's Inn as it was known when Robert Burns stayed here in 1787 and engraved his famous 'Stirling lines' on the window of his room much to the detriment of his later career. From here coaches set out daily or twice daily for Edinburgh and Glasgow. Here, well-to-do gentle visitors to the town could stay in expectation of the same sort of personal service that their own servants would provide at home.

Improved roads, safe for travel now that the country had been pacified after the Jacobite Rising, made movement between towns readily possible and improvements in horse-drawn transportation encouraged the local farmers and gentry and their families to travel to town. Here they could relax and enjoy the shopping and

The Golden Lion Hotel

the social life that buildings such as the Atheneum promised.

King Street demonstrates the first stage of urbanisation, where the older houses were demolished and replaced by newer and more desirable dwellings, and by contemporary building types neccessitated by the changing style of living.

New streets were also created in the hinterland of the burghal tofts especially at the north end of the town. Queen Street, Princes Street and Irvine Place all responded to the increase in the population as the town grew wealthier on the provision of services and the development of manufacturing.

Stretching from St Mary's Wynd to what is now Murray Place, Irvine Place is one of these Georgian inshots. The feus for the houses stipulated neat dwelling houses and offices of stone and lime with good blue slates, the houses to be two storeys high, set back eighteen feet from the road (i.e. have front gardens,

A classical terrace in Queen Street

somewhat of an innovation then), with dressed stone fronts and regular windows, the grounds to be developed as gardens or pleasure grounds. No 15 is a particularly grand example, being some three storeys high and pretentiously pedimented.

Queen Street, the next street along, dating from 1820, is clearly slightly lower class, the houses joined to form terraces' stepping down the hill. Enjoyable architecture, nevertheless, showing a subtle variety of door and window treatment within a simple classical format.

Georgian doorway in Allan Park

Development within the walls was not enough, however, and expansion began to take place along the roadways leading out of town. As already mentioned, the Barras Yett and the inner port were demolished, so too was the customs post on the bridge (to be replaced by the decorative obelisks visible today) and the cattle market was moved out to the edge of town, nearer the bridge. With settled times the need for physical protection had ceased and economic protection was also becoming a thing of the past. The Guildry and Incorporations also were losing their powers of monopoly with the introduction of burgess elections.

The road to the west, Port Street, was developed and beyond it Melville Place where grand merchants' villas began to rival those of the Tobacco Lords in Glasgow. In Port Street, today, access to a popular fruit shop is via the cobbled courtyard of another of Stirling's Georgian coaching inns. The former outbuildings clearly were used as craftsmen's workshops in Victorian times, and today the inn continues as a bar. Discovering this trace of the past is a bit of urban serendipity, a consequence of poking the nose into accessible places.

Across the street is a pleasant little pedimented house from the 1770s with parapet urns and a delicate asymmetrical front elevation. Next door is a house converted to shops at ground level, where a dentist's chambers with a wonderful 1940s art deco front door and canopy can be found. Surprisingly still intact, the door even has its original etched glass and the first-floor windows have attractive art deco iron balconettes for flower boxes.

Georgian villas beyond the Walls

VICTORIAN STIRLING

As the town grew, tall tenements with shops below began to appear. One interesting bar and restaurant is a contemporary 'Victorian' conversion, with modern 'open' plan, full of expensive, antique junk of the kind that creates atmosphere (and represents a sound investment for the owner).

Next door, Thomas Elders, in typical imported red brick, is a Victorian shop and office block where the 'Renaissance *palazzo parti* ' still survives as a useful architectural tool.   This time, however, the 'base' consists of shops with big plate-glass windows for commercial display, the piano nobile is two floors of showrooms disguised behind large residential Tudor bay windows, and, above, the 'attic' storey is offices, with ubiquitous Scottish dormers peeping over the gutter.   The historicist technique of designing building forms had obviously continued; indeed, it continues today to be helpful to architects struggling to make elevations.   The architect of Thomas Elder was also responsible for the adjacent Wolf's Craig building (1897-8) on the corner of Port Street and Dumbarton Road.   This is one of three fascinating buildings by this relatively unknown Victorian rogue architect called John Allan. He must have been particularly proud of this building, because he signed and dated it.

This shop and office block is designed in a free historic style, using stone, plate glass and red Welsh bricks all on a steel frame.   Allan also provided the building with its own electricity generator.   But look at how he subverts the style, and the bizarre composition of his extrordinary corner turret, and the almost comic sculptures.   One, which unfortunately looks more like a Pekinese, was intended to depict the wolf celebrated in the town's history as the creature which alerted a sentry to a Norse attack and was formerly included in the civic coat-of-arms. Another, the bull's head, is a reminder of personal interpretations of the heraldic shields and odd pithy quotations of baronial style.

The 'Square'in the Arcade

At each corner of the crossing are excellent examples of the way Victorian architects and their clients acknowledged the importance of place, recognising the crossing and designing up to suit it, making private their contribution to the architecture of the public domain.

Commercial vigour came faster with the railways.   In 1907 the first branch connection was made to the Scottish central line joining Stirling directly to both Edinburgh and Glasgow.   The present station, dating from 1915, is an engaging glass and iron confection, by James Millar of Weymss Bay Station fame. Here in Stirling is a similar low spacious concourse with a splendid curving overbridge across the lines, all hidden discreetly behind a pink baronial façade with only a little glass entrance canopy to hint at what glories lie behind.

Menzies' shop in King Street

Leading up to town is an interesting new street, inserted into the backlands to connect the then heart of the town, King Street, to bypass the Victorian Murray Place.   This is not any old (new) street, but a glass-covered new street - an arcade more serendipity;   this shopping street with all-glass façades, is roofed over to keep the rain off, and has in the centre an unexpected little covered square with a lettable public hall on the first floor now in use as a tea room. What an exciting affair this must have seemed when it was opened in 1881.

The present entrance to the arcade was originally to Temperance Hall, another great movement of the times. But, the John Menzies shop alongside is Victorian innovation at its gutsiest. Unashamedly made of cast-iron and plate-glass, it has wonderfully vulgar ovulate dormer windows and a great flat glazed façade. Its neighbours in the street, themselves otherwise bold contemporary interpretations of the Renaissance, pale into insignificance beside it.

In Friar's Street nearby, a rebuilding of the old Wynd leading to the Blackfriars Monastery, another exciting innovative building by John Allan can be found: more red brick and a radical rethink of the urban tenement, No 23 is balconied with large plate-glass windows and an eccentric Dutch gable. It displays Allan's predeliction for eccentric exhortations such as 'Do Yer Duty' and 'Honour Principle'. Quite a find

23 Friars Street

An Allan exhortation

The Clydesdale Bank on the corner of the Corn Market is another vigorous example of the tripartite parti; this time a rusticated arcaded base topped with a continuous mock balcony has a powerfully asymmetric piano nobile above, topped in turn by dormers and chimneys and, as a finale a Clydesdale horse disguised as a royal unicorn. It is an accomplished example of the genre.

This corner also signals a really significant intervention, Corn Exchange Market: a new street was struck out through the town walls to link the new suburb of Allan Park to the historic burgh centre.

Suburban arts and crafts villa

NEW SUBURBS

The Georgian overspill beyond the walls burgeoned, after Mar Park came Albert Road and Victoria Square, a planned grid-iron new town, streets designed for coach and carriage, for fresh air, the houses set back in sylvan plots splendid in baronial trim and noble random stone. Here pleasure can be had by watching how the passing of the century sees the classical gentility of the Dumbarton Road terraces and linked houses give way to the gothic grandeur of the late 1880s and ushers in the Edwardian exuberance of the arts and crafts.

The necessary cultural buildings demanded by an aspiring bourgeosie are found here in the West End, too. In Albert Place, the splendid Doric-porticoed Smith Art Gallery built in 1872 by John Lessels was the obligatory town museum; the Albert Hall (1883) opened with a performance of Handel's *Messiah*, is a Victorian Venetian palace by William Simpson, built to provide a house for music, generating in consequence operatic and choral societies while the Holy Trinity Church (1875), by Sir Robert Rowan Anderson, provides a home for the Episcopalians of the new suburb.

MUNICIPAL BUILDINGS

The public library (1904), financed by the Carnegie Trust, in Corn Exchange is a mishmash of Victorian historicism but across the street is a genuinely innovative building of the era: the new municipal buildings (1908) by J Gaffe Gillespie of Glasgow, who won the competition for itsdesign. Here is Edwardian architecture at its best. Full-blown confidence in the vocabulary of the Renaissance but inventive and demonstrating awareness of thecontemporary Free Style movement in its details. And inside, fittingly in a garrison town, decorative mosaic details in the

well-proportioned and spacious entrance hall celebrate the various Scottish regiments to which the town had been host. Confidence can be found here, in the effortless utilisation of the new technologies of iron, plate-glass and electricity in the interior.

Edwardian exuberance – the Municipal Buildings

The 1960s extension by the burgh architect is a decent-ish modern building saved from banality by the use of quality materials, pleasant landscaping and an appropriate touch of decoration in the commemorative wrought-iron panel of the Battle of Stirling Bridge. Inside, however, civic pride is lacking; Edwardian exuberance has been replaced by functional austerity and bureaucratic indifference.

Up historic Spittal Street can be found examples of complete nineteenth-century rebuilding, in quick succession: there is the gothic Snowdon School of 1855 with trefoil windows and a little spire; a classical temple (1825) housing the Forth Valley Health Board Headquarters (formerly Royal Infirmary); another classical temple, this time Erskine Church (1824-6) with a monument (1859) to the famous clergyman, Ebenezer Erskine, who brought about the partition of the Holy Rude Church; and beyond that again, in splendid silhouette, the county gaol (1847), with its turrets, battlements and fake lancet arrow loops, subsequently taken over by the military for use as a prison, and now looking for a client with a creative re-use for it.

A splendid example of such re-use can be found in the current conversion of the old high school into a tourist hotel within the historic confines of the burgh.

This high school was actually the third or fourth school.   First was the monastic school probably on this, the old franciscan site, then the school adjacent to Argyll Ludging, knocked down and rebuilt again, now a hotel, and then in 1854, a Liverpool firm of architects erected the first stages of this quadrangular collegiate school, the front and rear of the present group.

James MacLaren added a brilliant wing on Spittal Street in 1887, with a domed observatory on the four-storey tower, gifted by the local MP and Prime Minister, Sir Henry Campbell-Bannerman; and in an exuberant composition, the old Renaissance doorway from a late sixteenth-century house belonging to Adam Spittal, is set into a contemporary sculptured frame.

It remains only to have a quick look at the Victorian and later building up along Murray Place, the first of the by-pass roads. Here at the corner of Friar's Street is a charming little *art nouveau* shop at 1, 3 and 5 Moray Place, its pediment cut off crudely to allow a new fascia, looking for all the world like current smart Italian design. Across the street, No 64 is one of the most innovative and impressive tenements anywhere in Scotland; tall with attic storeys incorporating a great composition which includes a borrowing from Hawksmoor in the centre. Wonderful stuff—later architecture in Stirling is nowhere near as stylish.

Scotland's most impressive tenement

A disappointing, trivial Post-modern offering has just been erected to conceal the terrible gash in the fabric caused by the newest bypass, but, that said, the new Thistle Shopping Centre works because it is properly unseen, cleverly hidden by the existing street shops which open into it. The back destroys the town from the east but ivy and plenty of tall trees might help. More serendipity is the discovery inside of a bastion and dungeon from the old wall. Make a point of seeing it, experiencing simultaneously the past and the present.

STIRLING DEVELOPMENT

From its early founding in the twelfth century the burgh was an inward-looking society, closed, influencing only the surrounding countryside and controlling its trade and employment.

After the Union of the Crowns in 1707 and the abortive Jacobite Risings of 1715 and 45, Stirling ceased being a royal or even a significant town. The castle became a barracks and its noble rooms barracks quarters. A network of military roads was constructed to subdue the countryside. The Gaelic kingdom had been decisivley defeated for the last time and the future lay in overseas development and trade. Stirling became a local market town but in much closer contact with the rest of the world. First, with the turnpike roads came the coaches and travellers, and the town developed as a social centre for surrounding gentry in addition to its market function. With the railways came settlers, commuters whose money was earned elsewhere, but whose residence was in the burgh. Stirling became both an individual and more integrated part of a national urban style of living, developing into the town we see today.

VI
KELSO

Curious Twosomes and Stately Splendour

Kelso lies in the heart of the Scottish Border county only a few short miles from England. A burgh with long hard history of savage fighting and repeated destruction throughout the early years of its existence, particularly during the Scottish Wars of Independence, it owes its origin to the eleventh century establishment by David I of the Abbey of St Marys in Kelso, on the other bank of the 400 foot wide River Tweed from the now forgotten premier royal burgh of Scotland, Roxburgh. Unlike its earlier neighbour, Kelso survived these troubled times and prospered to become a busy market town with the largest lamb sales in Britain if not in Europe, and the biggest market square in Scotland.

The Square, Kelso

An unusual burgh in many respects, not least in the French feeling of its market square, Kelso is also a town of curious twosomes. It has two castles, Roxburgh and Floors, two rivers, the Tweed and the Teviot, two town squares, one hard and one soft and two swans, one black and one white. It also has two lamps from London's old Waterloo Bridge, two fascinating windows that conceal as much as they reveal and two buildings with most unusual models of themselves inside, not at all what you might expect. Even its Duke, the Duke of Roxburgh has two family trees.

111

THE ABBEY AT KELSO

Although Malcolm Canmore was the monarch who first united all Scotland, and under the influence of his English Queen, Margaret, initiated the consolidation of the kingdom through the advancement of the Roman Church, it was his son, King David I (1124-53) who developed a systematic policy of subjugation and control of the realm through the instruments of castle, kirk and burgh.

He had had the opportunity to observe and admire the operation of this Norman technique, the feudal system, during his long stay at the English court of his brother-in-law King Henry I, his sister Marjory or Maud was England's Queen. In 1113 on becoming Earl of Tweedale in his own right (he was already Earl of Huntingdon by marriage, and Baron of Cumbria at Henry's hand), David invited monks from the Benedictine Abbey of Tiron in Picardy, France, to establish a sister house at Selkirk, in his Earldom.

These Tironensians were a new order, founded only four years before, the first of the reformed Benedictine orders. It was unique in that each monk was a specialist artisan obliged by the rules of the order to practice a useful craft or art. There is little doubt that in the invitation to Selkirk what David had in mind was the improvement of his inheritance.

He had recognised that the Roman Catholic Church in England was a useful instrument of popular control and that its monastic orders had many useful skills to offer, including new ways of building and methods of scientific farming which would be important in his programme of modernisation.

When David returned to Scotland as king in 1124 he brought with him noble Norman friends to help him 'plant' the feudal system throughout his realm. He also removed his Tironensian monks from Selkirk to Kelso, where they would be next door to the new royal castle and burgh of Roxburgh ('rex burgh' or the king's burgh) which he intended as his principal seat in Scotland. His laws were to be enforced by sheriffs each in a royal castle, many of them Norman friends who owed their allegiance and their appointment to him. The preaching of the Roman Church would establish a common social and religious system and learning would be spread by the new monasteries founded by his royal decree. This strategy was to be financed by taxation of the nobility, by private donations to the church and, above all, by revenues from his newly chartered royal burghs which would also generate trade and industry throughout the country. All this, he believed, would bring to Scotland the higher standards of living and the relatively peaceful unity already enjoyed in England.

ABBEY

Under David's royal patronage, by 1128 Kelso had become the first abbey of the kingdom. Its Benedictine abbots, later mitred by the Pope to be the equal of

Scotland's bishops, played an important part in the development of a Scottish church independent from that of England, as well as in the creation of an efficient Scottish administration, many of the abbots became chancellors. Unfortunately the vulnerable strategic situation of Roxburgh with its castle and Kelso Abbey so close to the English border and the principal road from and to England ultimately assured their destruction in the Wars of Independence.

Kelso Abbey

What little is now left of the abbey is nevertheless the most complete fragment of a major Romanesque or Norman church in all Scotland. It follows the High Romanesque or Norman pattern of Ely and Cluny, having two transepts or crossings; one, still remaining, near the entrance and the other, now long gone, at the junction of the choir and the nave. The ruins of the north transept give a clear impression of what this great church must have been like. Seen from the burgh, a great multi-storey wall rears up, with three rows of superimposed round-headed windows. High, dominant, tower-like gables terminate the transept and nave, while, internally,

A ruined arch–Kelso Abbey

decorative arcading and geometric patterns enliven the wall surfaces, suggesting the assured work of master craftsmen. The doorways are deeply recessed, the arches enriched with mouldings and superimposed arcading and decorated pediments over. The door in the transept was used by the laity approaching from the burgh which had grown up at the gates of the abbey close. The great west doorway, or Galilee Porch, was reserved for ceremonial occasions when the monks would enter the church and approach the altar in procession. Two stones, found in the rediscovered graveyard of Roxburgh's St James Church, were placed here early in the nineteenth-century.

In its own time this magnificent building was living proof of the majesty of the Latin Church and of the Christian values of David's kingdom.

Sadly, the English determination to subjugate Scotland, to assimilate it into England as it had Wales, and the Scottish national will to resist, to remain free, which transcended the narrow territorial ambitions of the Norman and Celtic nobility saw Kelso Abbey - like the abbeys at Dryburgh, Jedburgh and Melrose - ravaged again and again till eventually, it was no longer fit for occupation.

Kelso Abbey was burned and finally brought low by the Earl of Hereford in the famous 'rough wooing' of 1545, when twelve monks and ninety laymen who had held out in the tower until it was shattered, were violently put to death. Fifteen years later what little was left of the Abbey was again looted and the monks forced to abandon it for ever.

CASTLE

The story of Roxburgh Castle is similar to that of the medieval abbey, a tale of constant strife and changing occupation, culminating in the total destruction, not only of the castle but of the burgh as well. Roxburgh, however, was finally and thoroughly destroyed by the Scots themselves.

King David had established his burgh next to the castle which had been strategically sited to dominate important river crossings on the Tweed and the Teviot. The Tweed is 400 feet wide at this point and these crossings were the first inland from Berwick, the strongly fortified port which commanded the border where it met the sea. Berwick was also the out-port for the vital Scottish wool trade and Roxburgh and Kelso were important markets in a fertile farming area which could feed and provision armies and provide them with horses, natural military targets.

Of the castle itself only a few fragments of masonry can now be seen atop the Marchidun or Marchmount, an 80 foot high, hilly outcrop between the two rivers, a naturally strong defensive position as its name suggest. This paucity of remains relates in particular to the accidental death of James II at a siege of the castle in 1460, at that time the last English-held stronghold in Scotland. While watching his gunners in action, one of the Scottish siege guns burst its casing and a flying fragment fatally wounded the King (another early example of the famous Scottish 'own goal'). In rage and grief the Scots, commanded by James' Queen Mary over ran the castle and the burgh razing them so ferociously that to this day no trace whatsoever of the burgh has been found.

James' infant son was crowned in the abbey, just several days after the King's death, the Earl Douglas himself placing the crown on the head of James III and defying anyone to remove it.

In 1564 James III granted the ruins and the castle lands to Walter Kerr of Cessford whose own fortified house was just a few miles away. After the Reformation the Kerrs also acquired the lands of the abbey, becoming Earls and

Dukes of Roxburgh. The present Duke, Sir Guy David Innes, the 10th Duke, whose seat, Floors Castle, is clearly visible across the Tweed from the Marchmount, is a descendant by marriage of that Walter Kerr and of the Earls of Innes; hence his two family trees.

BURGH

Before looking at Floors in detail perhaps the burgh itself should receive some attention. Kelso Abbey, on the other side of the wide river from Roxburgh, attracted gradually a group of dwellings related to the servicing of the abbey and the development of its markets. By the middle of the fifteenth-century when Roxburgh Castle and the burgh were finally destroyed, Kelso was a well-established bishop's (abbot's) burgh. There seems clear evidence that by then there was an easter Kelso at the abbey gates and around its mill, and a wester Kelso, with a mercat cross situated near the ferry on the Edinburgh Road.

A long High Street ran parallel the riverbank, from the mercat cross and ferry at the west end of the town to the abbey and another ferry at the east. The monks' mill lay in between at a point where a large caul or mill weir channelled the river flow on to its wheel; behind it, inland across the High Street lay stockyards where sheep and cattle were marshalled, and Scottish armies too.

Despite repeated despoliation in the interminable wars, Kelso flourished, surviving the Reformation too, and in 1634 became a Burgh of Barony in favour of the Kerrs of Cessford who had already been granted the castle lands

Kelso survived yet further setbacks. In the middle of the seventeenth-century, the old town suffered a calamitous fire (1645) which started with the burning of the house of plague victims, and spread uncontrollably. If this was not enough, just forty years later, in 1684 fire once again broke out and reduced the town to ashes, this time almost totally. The burgh appealed to the Privy Council for help as rebuilding was beyond its resources, and money for Kelso was raised all over Scotland.

It is probable that it was at this time that Kelso took its present shape. A market square, resembling a French place was developed where the stockyards had been, a tolbooth, with a spire and a clock, was built where the town hall now stands; and the burgh began to develop inland, away from the river, along Horsemarket and Woodmarket and the new Edinburgh Road. Slezer's view of Kelso just ten years later seems to suggest that rebuilding was prompt and that the greater part of the town was constructed adjacent to the abbey, rather than as before, spread out along the river. This is borne out by the later dates of the houses at the west end of Roxburgh Street as this end of the High Street is now known.

FLOORS CASTLE

The Kerrs of Cessford, became Earls of Roxburghe in time, and moved their family seat to Kelso, the centre of their now expanded estates; a newer and more convenient house was built on a riverside site facing the ruins of Roxburgh Castle using stone from Cessford Castle and the old friary of St Peters in Roxburgh.

In 1721 this house appears to have been substantially rebuilt to provide a fitting seat for the 5th Earl who had become the 1st Duke (in recognition of his position as Secretary of State for Scotland).

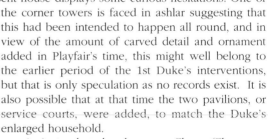

Floors Castle

The exterior of the present house displays some curious hesitations. One of the corner towers is faced in ashlar suggesting that this had been intended to happen all round, and in view of the amount of carved detail and ornament added in Playfair's time, this might well belong to the earlier period of the 1st Duke's interventions, but that is only speculation as no records exist. It is also possible that at that time the two pavilions, or service courts, were added, to match the Duke's enlarged household.

As it stands today, however, Floors (Fleurs, on old maps) is very much the work of W. H. Playfair (1789-1857), the fashionable Edinburgh architect. He had been selected in 1841 by the 6th Duke, who inheriting the title at the age of twenty-one, and much under the influence of the writings of Sir Walter Scott, wished to embellish or medievalise his county seat.

The young Duke and Playfair created a marvellous confection of turrets, towers and domes, the word confection being a very appropriate term in this case, as the basement of the chateau houses a wonderful sugar-icing and matchstick model of the house made for the the top of the Duke's birthday cake in 1851, the year of the Chrystal Palace and the Great Exhibition.

A carved detail at the Castle

Playfair's energetic additions centred on the roof where a great carved and crenellated battlement forms a strong base to support an effervescence of chimneys, finials, turrets and towers, ogee domes and gaping gargoyles which create a dream landscape high among the clouds.

Floors Castle roofscape

Approaching Floors today movie buffs might just recognise it as 'Greystoke', Tarzan's childhood home in the film of that name.

Inside, a sequence of south-facing rooms overlook the lawns and the river. These are magnificently appointed and display splendid tapestries, rich furnishings, objects of vertu, paintings and family portraits.

The magnificent drawing room and the impressive grand ballroom beyond are much later in date than might be thought, and are the creation of May, the 8th Duchess, who altered them after the turn of this century. Daughter of a New York banker, she brought to Floors her superb collection of French tapestries and furniture and set about creating a fitting setting to display them. She removed Playfair's elaborate but heavy mock Jacobean ceilings, and walled off his huge bay window at the end of the ballroom to make a place to show off the older family portraits and her Jacobean tapestries, a fitting feature in her view, to close the long vista of the

sequential grand apartments.

The Duke's birthday cake model

Her tastes were not always for the antique, however, and in the little Needle Room between the two apartments, reputedly modelled on a room in Versailles, can be found paintings by Matisse and other contemporary post-impressionist artists.

Fine as these rooms are, admiration is constrained a little by the realisation that, around the time Duchess May was causing decorative fireplaces to be carved in the manner of Grinling Gibbons, Charles Rennie Mackintosh was building his wonderful white modern houses, only a hundred miles away on the banks of the Clyde.

Floors Castle roof

117

In front of the house, beyond the impressive ha-ha an elaborate sunk ditch and wall which keep the cows off the lawn, a holly tree near the bank of the Tweed is said to mark the spot where in 1460, James II was killed. True or not it is a good spot from which to consider further the mystery of Kelso's two vanished burghs.

First, Roxburgh, David I's premier burgh, which gave its name to the county; and second, Sir James Vanbrugh, the Architect Royal, to whom the design of Floors Castle has traditionally been attributed.

In the case of Roxburgh nothing of its buildings has ever been found. Were the very foundations removed to ensure the English would never return or does it lie hidden elsewhere.

It has long been held that when the 1st Duke (and 8th Earl) had had the original Floors built to honour his new dukedom, he was advised by Sir John Vanbrugh (1664-1726), the Architect Royal. At the time of his elevation the Duke,

as Secretary for Scotland, was living at the Court in London, where he would undoubtedly have known both of Vanbrugh and his work. In the drawing room an early painting by William Wilson of the original Floors shows a house not unlike Eastbury Park (1718-38) by Vanbrugh and the layout of Floors certainly has a strong baroque parti, not dissimilar to that often employed by Vanbrugh.

Recent revisionist opinion or resurgent Scottish National chauvinism, now attributes

The Castle before Playfair's additions

the entire design to William Adam (1689-1748), the father of the more famous Robert who was certainly entrusted with the masonry contract, his first on such a large scale. Later he claimed authorship of the entire design in his *Vitruvius Scotticus* but is this likely, would this not also have been his first major architectural commission, and as such, surely noteworthy?

Unfortunately any evidence as to the truth was sadly lost in a fire in the castle records office in the last century.

There is some similar doubt about resposibility for the design of nearby Broomlands, another house in Kelso also built by William Adam around the same time as Floors. Though badly spoiled by insensitive nineteenth-century additions, bay windows, porch and parapet, not to mention additional bays added to the south, this house was clearly a very simple Georgian county house to begin with.

The present main entrance to Floors estate is another of the Duchess' interventions, built in 1929 by Reginald Fairlie, who also designed her monument to her husband and his forbears, the Memorial Cloister and Garden adjacent to the front of the abbey in Bridge Street (1933). Where the gateway is an impressive exercise in French Renaissance, with electronically operated gates, the cloister sited next to the abbey is Gothic in character with a strong overlay of Celticism in the column capitals and the bosses; the Duchess and her architect obviously favoured the same historicist eclecticism as Prince Charles does today.

The cloister incorporates a thirteenth-century doorway from the original chapter house. Another exercise in eclecticism is the adjacent War Memorial (1921) by Sir Robert Lorimer; built to commemorate the First World War dead, it takes the form of a late medieval mercat cross, but the saint figure is that of England's patron saint, Saint George. The influence of May, Duchess of Roxburghe, and historical distortion is thus manifest at both ends of Kelso's long High Street.

The War Memorial and Abbey beyond

Carved Detail–the Dukes' Mausoleum

HIGH STREET

Nowadays the street is broken up in name at least into three different parts.

ROXBURGH STREET

Roxburgh Street is the first of these stretching from the gatehouse at the west end to the square in the middle.

Midway along from the castle gates to the square, is one of Kelso's architectural tours de force, the original Free Church built in 1856 by F. T. Pilkington (1832-98), the architect of the better-known Barclay Church (1863) in Edinburgh. Like that church, St John's, Edenside, is highly individualistic in its manner. The tower is a unique free composition making it a striking landmark in town, seen from as far away as the Teviot Bridge.

At first glance, the church seems to be quite simple, a straightforward Victorian Gothic pile. A less cursory examination, however, reveals not only a curious, balanced asymmetry and a huge entrance porch that isn't - the real entrance is via a smaller door in the side alley above - but an extraordinary exaggeration of Gothic cusping that finishes up Saracenic in feeling rather than Christian. A tight budget, perhaps, might also explain why the carving is found only at the front; it even stops abruptly at the back of the porch, column and on the side elevations. This is a building meant to be seen only from the front.

Pilkington's Church

The interior is also notable for its spatial and structural complexity, sitting over a parish hall lit via the spurious front porch. Definitely an enthusiast's item this, as is the wonderfully complex little workshop and yard next door in Bowmont Street, an ingenious Victorian workshop and yard well worthy of preservation .

Nearly opposite the church on the riverside is a little modern house of the late 1960s using traditional materials in a most untraditional way built by Peter Womersley. No 106 is the old Kelso Dispensary or hospital, an innovatory building in its day which served the burgh from 1777 till the recent setting up of the Maxwellheugh Cottage Hospital.

No 66 is the old Tweedsdale Physical and Antiquarian Society building of 1834, while another pair of interesting houses are No 48, a late eighteenth-century classical villa with wings, and Walton Hall, named after Izaak, a simple, single-storey house on the riverside built in 1820 as a fishing lodge for Walter Scott's school friend and publisher, John Ballantyne. It has a Doric porch and is built in harled rubble with exposed dressings and a piended slate roof. Stables at the rear are linked to the house by walls and cast-iron railings. A boundary wall and gateway add dignity to the house.

Towards the square there are some interesting shopfronts with Tuscan pilasters and a brass horseshoe in the middle of the road marks where Bonnie Prince Charlie's horse cast a shoe in 1746, when he and his army occupied the town. He is reported to have remarked he had more drinking friends in Kelso than fighting ones. This was not the first visit by a Jacobite army, as in the 1715 Rising, a Highland army under Brigadier Mackintosh occupied the town, proclaiming the Old Pretender rightful King of Scotland, England, France and Ireland, to cries of 'No Union', 'No Malt Tax'. On neither occasion does the town seem to have suffered much except from unpaid bills for billeting, by friend and foe alike.

The High Street continues into and across the square, alongside an interesting block of shops and houses with a pilastered upper story and a recent replica Georgian shop for a building society at ground floor.

BRIDGE STREET

Beyond the square it is renamed Bridge Street, and leads off towards the abbey and the bridge beyond. It has a number of good eighteenth-century Georgian buildings here. On the left-hand side, No 20 is a house of the grander type with its pediment and rusticated quoins, now spoiled a little by a crudely inserted shopfront. Between it and a stylish Victorian gothic office and shop block is a little 'Johnny aa' shop inserted in an old lane or vennel.

The Spread Eagle and the Queen's Head are two of Kelso's old coaching inns, which, like the Cross Keys, date from the days when Kelso was the first stop on the journey from Edinburgh to Newcastle. The Queen's Head is quite striking in its black-and-white colour scheme, with accentuated architectural dressings, and faces across the street into the newish gateway to Ednam House, a fine Georgian house to which we shall return.

Adjacent to this gate, No 9 has the distinction of being the first house to be lit by electricity in Scotland in February 1818. The then proprietor was William Muir, a copper-smith. On the other side of the gateway is a foreign architectural intrusion in Kelso, a Tudor block of shops and offices, quite alien in effect. Nos 21-25 are interesting Victorian cast-iron shopfronts. While at the end of Bridge Street toward the abbey is a rather elegant little block of shops with delicate, rather stylish Ionic columns, appropriate perhaps at an entrance to a ducal town.

ABBEY COURT

Down to the right, Abbey Court as it is now called, is the tail of the old High Street which led to the first bridge (and the older ferry). Here are some good eighteenth and nineteenth-century vernacular houses and an older, seventeenth-century building, Turret House, which may well be one of the early stone houses in the town, built after the great fire of 1684. The front is dominated by a prominent turnpike stair topped by a square crow-stepped cap house. The earliest part of this

The Turret House, now a museum was once a sweetie shop

house appears to have been built as a boatman's cottage, a lintel dated may well be from that stage of building, later the cottage was enlarged and the stair added. Over the centuries this picturesque little building has accommodated in turn, a ferryman, a schoolmaster, a miller, a tailor, a skinner, a minister and in the 1930s a sweetie shop. Today it is a fascinating local museum which also gives some idea of what a seventeenth-century burgher's house might have been like.

Across the road is the Scottish Episcopal Church of St Andrew, built in 1868-9 to the design of Sir Robert Rowand Anderson, the architect of the Central Station Hotel in Glasgow and the McEwan Hall in Edinburgh. Built in multicoloured sandstone, mainly red with lighter dressings, it has an elegant and interesting conical Gothic spire, seen to good advantage from the bridge, with a charming *St Andrew's* carved floral roundel enclosing a bust of a very Victorian St Andrew. It sits between *Church* Ednam House boundary wall and the river, above the abutments of the old bridge

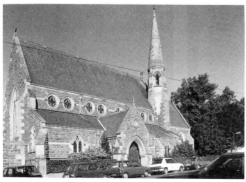

where a Tweedometer can still be seen, a measuring scale giving the river heights (of great interest to salmon fishermen, and at times of flood).

The interior is finely detailed in the high Victorian ecclesiastical style with a stenciled chancel ceiling and pulpit, interesting modern stained glass windows and a collection of monuments from an earlier church (1769) which formerly stood on the site. These include a weeping figure (1844) on the 'gothic' tomb of John Robertson of Ednam House and a contemporary sculptured reredos with scenes from the life of St Andrew. The panelling of the inner porch and frontal case are from the demolished chapel at the hirsel. Alongside the church are the original gates of Ednam House and a pleasantly landscaped early nineteenth-century terrace.

BRIDGES

The Kelso Bridge, another of the burgh's architectural gems, is described in the statistical account of Scotland (1839) as by far 'the most perfect specimen of modern architecture in the Parish'. It was built in 1803 to replace an earlier bridge of 1754 which had been carried away by a great flood and was the first major bridge commission of John Rennie (1761-1821) who later became one of Scotland's most famous civil engineers.

The bridge was most innovatory for its time, featuring the first-ever use of flat three-centred arches to avoid any unnecessary rise in the height of the bridge, an important point for horse-drawn traffic. Rennie's later and more famous Waterloo Bridge in London was based on Kelso Bridge as a model, a fact commemorated by two lampposts on the south side and brought there when that bridge was demolished in 1935. Rennie also built London Bridge and Southwark Bridge and went on to build canals, docks and bridges throughout the whole of Britain (even the Bell Lighthouse), and also built overseas in Sweden and Portugal.

One of the lamps on Waterloo Bridge

An elegant, five-arched structure, Kelso Bridge displays stylish paired Roman Doric columns between the arches and features rusticated stonework with large accented keystones and a blocked balustrade. Almost 500 feet long (494 feet) and 57 feet high with a 25 feet wide roadway, it has a pleasantly deceptive scale, seeming smaller and less bulky than these dimensions suggest.

The Kelso Bridge (1805) was John Rennie's first major commission

Legend has it that the groove along the parapet was caused by the constant scraping of the penny for the toll by reluctant toll payers, hence the name the 'grudging groove'. A riot occurred in 1854 when a demand to publish the toll accounts was not met, the mob sawed down the toll gate and threw it in the Tweed, the toll-keeper himself lending them a candle to grease the saw.

The toll-keeper's cottage at the town end of the bridge turns out to be a handsome three-storey house when seen from the riverside, while at the other end an elegant triumphant arch is all that is left of the old entrance to Springwood Park, designed by the Edinburgh architect, James Gillespie Graham (1777-1855) in 1882, who also designed the now vanished Springwood Mansion, the home of the Douglases of Springwood, whose arms may be seen in the parish church.   Markets and shows are now held in Springwood Park, with three important shows in July: Kelso Ram Sales, the biggest in Scotland; the Ponies of Britain Show; and the Border Union Show.

Another, slightly earlier bridge nearby, also featuring columns, is William Elliot's 1798 bridge over the Teviot Friar's Cottage, near the site of the old Roxburgh friary of St Peters. It has a ramped approach as it employs the old fashioned single-centre arch.

SQUARE

Returning to the town centre, we find Kelso's most distinctive feature: the square.   This is the largest market square anywhere in Scotland, with a reminder of former days, an iron bull ring, still set in the centre, above a vault housing a box containing coins and newspapers and other souvenirs, only opened up at each successive coronation to add more.

The impressive town hall in the centre was built originally by public subscription in 1816 to replace a decaying thatched tolbooth and tower.   Its appearance today, however, with its elaborate entrance columns and coat of arms over the door, dates from a later Edwardian alteration of 1905 when the piazza, the original ground-floor arches, was filled in, and the interior lavishly revamped.

Towards the abbey, which is visible through a narrow gap between the buildings, the eastern side of the square is bounded by an interesting tenement block of the 1770s with shops below and splendid palladian-style windows above, which, on closer scrutiny, turn out to be rather subtle, concealing more than they reveal.   The central arched portion in each case reveals itself to be a blind panel masking the floor of the room above, suggesting thereby a superior piano nobile or principal floor of a grander house–an amusing visual conceit.

The Town Hall

Alongside this Georgian building are two bank buildings: one in twentieth-century 'repro Georgian' (1934) with red tiles and overhanging eaves which would look more at home in an English market town; the other is genuine early Victorian, built originally for the British Linen Bank.

The other side of the Square is dominated by the grand Cross Keys Hotel, a famous Georgian coaching inn with a Victorian upper storey and a modern shopping centre where it once stabled fifty horses. It was originally built in 1761 for John Dickson, a Kelso lad who fled to London to avoid punishment for breaking the lantern over the town well and returned home after making his fortune as a naval agent and a privateer in Havana, to build the inn and Ednam House, the finest Georgian mansion

The blind window

in the district. He had bought the estate and nearby village of Ednam but opted to live in some grandeur in the town from which he had fled in shame. He chose as the architect for his house and his hotel, a local man, James Nisbet.

EDNAM HOUSE

One of Kelso's unexpected glories, sited on the north bank of the Tweed, Ednam House (1761), formerly known as Havana House, enjoys a splendid prospect across the river and the valley. Now a fishing hotel, and fortunately thus open to the public, it contains the most unexpectedly wonderful interiors featuring marvellous executed plaster ceilings, finer and grander than anything in the nearby castle, and certainly unusual in Scotland at that time. The ceilings are different in each room. In the lounge, the original Georgian salon, Apollo is portrayed in his chariot chasing Aurora across the sky; the four elements - earth, air, fire and water - are represented at the

corners; and extracts from Aesop's Fables illustrated round the edges. Apollo's head re-appears carved in the centre of the carrera marble fireplace.

In what must have been a music room or library the central panel features

Ednam House, formerly Havana House

the decorative arts, painting, sculpture and music while featured in the dining room or drawing room on the opposite side, Europa and the Bull can be found inset in base relief in the wall above a splendid coloured marble fireplace. The upper landing is a splendid *tour de force* designed as a little top-lit temple with delicate columns and a fine cupola.

The doors throughout the house, too, are also imaginatively detailed and well preserved. Made of hardwoods from Havana, all with their original brass locks, handles and hinges they are beautifully kept and a pleasure to look at.

The house also contains a fine collection of local topographic paintings including an Alexander Nasmyth (1758-1840), Scotland's first landscape painter, showing the earlier bridge. The founder's portrait in the hall is a recent copy of a portrait in Greenwich Hospital but elsewhere are representations of the seventeenth-century Tolbooth Square, and of the bridge as well as

Detail from a fireplace

some interesting early photographs of Kelso. The proprietor has an interesting album and a theory that the house may have been designed by one of the English Wyatts.

A splendid Georgian gothic garden house can be found on the lawns overlooking the river. Recently sensitively altered, it terminates the vista from the bridge, on the way in from Abbey Court where a replica gateway gives some impression of the former grandeur of the house and its original approaches.

Ednam House Hotel, as it is now called, is currently entered via a new gateway cut through from Bridge Street on the site of the old town tron or weighbridge.

MARKETS

Returning to the square, facing the town hall two streets lead off; on either side these are two of the markets - Kelso has three adjacent to or running off the square.

The unusual house on the square at one end of Woodmarket has been noted already, but No 23 is an interesting building with an elaborately carved façade featuring female heads, cornucopias and cherubs. Formerly a seedsman's warehouse, it is now a bank. The Corn Exchange was built in 1885 and had seventy-one stalls inside and a musicians' gallery for social occasions, a reminder of the high quality of provincial life before television.

The Coal Market lies at the north end of Woodmarket and extends through Cross Street to join Horsemarket. The building ahead is the former Roxy cinema built in 1793; its ecclesiastical origins can still be seen in lancet windows along its flank walls.

Running back to the square, Horsemarket is mostly of nineteenth-century origin with an Edwardian post office and some pleasant Georgian shops. A modern housing infill is ingeniously concealed behind the left-hand side and one of the nearby fast-food shops has a picturesque three-dimensional carved fish and chip sign which adds a little vigour to this rather strait-laced street. Its relaxed appearance is marred only by a crass 1960s supermarket on the right-hand side. Will it too aquire a period flavour in time? Across the road the Black Swan, a somewhat typical nineteenth-century bar with the usual expedient modern alterations, offers an opportunity for an interesting 'pub-crawl'.

Kelso's two swans are two bars virtually sited back to back. An urban explorer's route leads the visitor from Horsemarket Street into the Black Swan, through it and out again into Woodmarket, across it and into the White Swan, and through it in turn into the graveyard (is this a beer to bier walk?) and across into the Queen's Head, through it too and out into Bridge Street, from which a final short stroll takes the explorer into Ednam House's striking interior and out on to the lawns on the riverbank with a splendid view of the bridge and the flat land across the river where the St Jane's Fair was traditionally held. All this for the architectural effects, of course.

Round about this old part of town are a number of interesting streets and backlands. In any burgh these old streets have names which suggest former activities and customs and Kelso is no exception. Butts is the street along the top of the graveyard – clearly a relic of the days of the wappenshaws when burghers owed a duty of watch and ward and had to possess arms and armour as well as turning out for compulsory drills. Butts' suggests bow and arrow practice on the church green.

Oven Wynd is a reminder of earlier days when not all houses in a burgh would necessarily have a fire for everyday cooking. Wood was a scarce commodity which had to be cut and brought into the town, hence Woodmarket. Bakers and piemen provided a public cooking service in those times. Drying House Lane is a relic of Kelso's brief foray into the home-grown tobacco industry.

A pend in 51 Roxburgh Street, at the bottom end of Union Street, leads into a blacksmith's forge which used to be Kelso's Ragged School. Near here is another turn-of-the-century building with a corner turret and crow-stepped gables, the Red Lion, in which some interesting arts and crafts stained glass and interesting timber details can be seen.

At the other end of Union Street across Bowmont Street, a splendid public library (1905) by Peddie & Washington Brown has an interesting wrought-iron gateway and some fine lettering in a sculpted panel over the door. Built in ashlar with large Jacobean windows, elaborate curvilinear gablets and a green slate roof and with an interesting trussed interior, it is a good example of contemporary architecture of the arts and crafts movement.

Just beyond it at the junction of Bowmont Street and East Bowmont Street stands Trinity North Church (1885), by John Stanforth who built Greyfriars Church in Dumfries. This church has a complex front elevation, featuring unusual skewed transepts, circular stair towers and a tall tower with a corner turret. It looks rather picturesque, among its trees, but what a pity the town has been so disrupted by demolition here to make way for the ubiquitous car parks

PARISH CHURCHES

Kelso has two, large adjacent open spaces in the centre - a most unusual feature in a Scottish town. The square (the mercat square) is setted, busy and noisy, enlivened by colourful window boxes and plant tubs which have won it awards.

The graveyard or 'Church Square', by contrast, is green, tree-ed, grassed and quiet, trees and peace, a restful almost hushed haven. Obviously the original Abbey Close, now a sylvan enclave, it contains the abbey ruins, Lorimer's War Memorial and the Memorial to Dukes of Roxburghe as well as the parish church, an interesting octagonal building with, inevitably it would seem in Kelso, two front doors.

Kelso's parish church as an institution, is old, a church of St Mary and St John existed even before the founding of the abbey in 1128, and was granted to the

The Parish Church

abbey in its charter, as the site for the new foundation. After the Reformation the parish replaced a part of the nave as a church and in the balcony, a school. However, in 1773 the roof collapsed and James Nisbet, the architect of Ednam House, was invited to design a new parish church. Looking at it now, it is hard to believe that just 150 years ago the town guide described this church as 'a misshapen pile, without exception the ugliest and least suitable architecture of all the parish churches of Scotland'. Tastes have certainly changed. The local nickname for the church is the 'mustard pot' and with its pyramidal roof, topped by a little cupola, you can see why. The octagonal plan of the church is not uncommon in the

egalitarian Presbyterian church having been strongly advocated by John Wesley while the little belfry above the older front porch houses the ancient abbey bells, moved there when their situation in the ruinous abbey tower had become dangerous.

Externally the church is built of rubble sandstone with dressed margins to the windows, rows of round-headed windows at gallery level (two per side) and smaller hooded windows at ground floor, both linked by string courses at sill level. A two-storey porch and a stair, with a little belfry over, faces the town, but there is another entrance on the far side with an internal stair

Sometimes
alled the
mustard pot'

and the vestry to one side. Here can be found an unusual collecting box in the shape of a model of the church, securely chained to the wall.

When originally built the church had a domed interior, a simple Georgian pulpit and elegant, understated, private boxes. Each trade had a box on the church floor, upstairs was reserved for the Duke of Roxburghe and his family in the centre and the local laird, Douglas of Springwood, whose coat of arms can be seen on the face of the gallery, to one side.

Increasing demand for instrumental music led to a remodelling of the pulpit in 1904, to include an organ.

In the inner hall a photograph of the church interior before the Victorian *The interior*

improvements hangs on the wall, and inside the colours of the Kelso Yeomanry, and of the Household Cavalry, record an association of the Dukes of Roxburghe with the church and with the Regiment. These latter colours were placed there in 1928, by permission of King George, at the behest of the Duke and his brother. The present organ was installed in 1964 to replace a harmonium, placed there in 1901 on the very day of Queen Victoria's death.

Sir Walter
Scott

Insignia of two of the Incorporated Trades–hammermen and shoemakers–also hang on the wall, a reminder of the days when each trade had its own box pew in the church. Communion tokens can also be seen on the sanctual rail while a memorial tablet on the wall commemorates all the Protestant ministers of the church, starting with Paul Knox (1574-1576), nephew of the great Reformer himself, who must be spinning in his grave at the thought that the present incumbent is one of that 'monstrous regiment of women', the Revd Marian Dodds. Paul Knox was an Episcopalian from Norwich; the first genuine Scots Presbyterian minister was the Revd William Jack in 1687. The church records go back to the times when attendance at church was obligatory on all residents and fines were levied for staying at home.

Over beyond the far corner of the graveyard towards the Knowes, the Waverley Lodge is an interesting Victorian house incorporating an earlier cottage where Walter Scott stayed with his relatives in 1783 when he briefly attended Kelso Grammar School in the days when Lancelot Whale was the Rector. A bust of the author is displayed on a bracket on the gables to the street, and a statue of his dog lies over the garden entrance.

SCHOOL

Like all Scottish burghs, Kelso had a high school, starting life as the grammar school, Roxburgh, passing to the abbot of Kelso in 1152 and mentioned in 1156 as one of the four principal high schools of Scotland, along with Edinburgh, Perth and Stirling. Following the Reformation and the dissolution of the Abbey, the School was taken over by the burgh and re-established in a loft of the choir. In 1656 the children were given twenty days holiday, extended to four weeks in 1673; schooling, at that time, being for boys only.

In 1780 a new building was built alongside in the abbey grounds to house the English scholars, the old school continuing to hold those studying the classics and in 1820 a completely new building was built known as Kelso Grammar School.

Kelso's school thus has a history of some seven centuries of continuous development and has numbered among its pupils Sir Walter Scott and James and John Ballantyne who became his publishers and whose bankrupcy caused him such stress. Burns visited the school in 1787 on his tour of the Borders. A new public school (1879), built in Abbey Row, recently became a community centre, the site itself being thought to have been a former plague burial ground. All the Kelso schools were reorganised in 1929 as Kelso High School when the old Kelso High School, built in Edenside Road in 1878, was replaced by a splendid new building in Bowmore Road.

TWENTIETH CENTURY

The high school is one of Kelso's unexpected serendipities, a vintage 1930s building built to unite all the Kelso schools. Its architects were a young partnership, Reid & Forbes, who had won the Leith Academy competition in 1928, going on to build Inverness Academy and then Kelso High School (1936). The building

The High School

belongs to that period in Scotland when, in the aftermath of the Great Depression, things had started to look up again. Like Thomas Tait at St Andrew's House and his more famous Empire Exhibition, the architects of the school have adopted some of the formal qualities of the Modern movement in architecture, crossing them in a typically 'cautious' Scottish way with elements of traditional architectural ornament and formal composition and paying lip-service, too, to fasionable ornament of the *art deco* period. The high school has the long extended lines made possible by steel and reinforced concrete, horizontal steel windows, and a light-hearted, light-coloured, cheerfulness. The flat modelled ornament is a source of enjoyment and delight and the vertical tower with its projection piers and clock is a reminder of the art of composition, of arranging the parts of a building, not by chance, or from functional expediency, but in accordance with aesthetic theories of form. A sculptured war memorial tablet plays its part in enriching the civic quality of the school. The building seems to be reasonably well cared for, perhaps even cherished. This building should be compared with the Broomlands Primary School as an expression of the values of its time, just fifty odd years ago when civic quality was expected in a public building.

The Broomland Primary School is a typical building of the 1970s and 1980s, a standard industrial building, a shed adapted as a primary school. It is practical and functional but its undistinguished form lacks either excitment or dignity, and though it will probably be a cheerful enough place to teach or learn in, civic values are unlikely to be inculcated and expectations of architecture will be minimal. It is saved by its background of trees, a long-term gesture to the future by a Georgian estate owner.

In contrast to the impressive high school, this building is a cheap standard building which a change of graphics could turn into a supermarket or a car saleroom. It is visible evidence of a changing attitude to building and to education.

I think it is characteristic of a ruthless and money-oriented society. Where in this building could one site a war memorial? Where is the long-term gesture, like the background of Georgian tree-planting which sets it off so well?

There are two other interesting recent modern buildings in Kelso. First, the striking Civic Trust Award-winning Edenside Surgery in Inch Road built by Peter Womersley in 1967, extended recently to create a Community Health Centre. The surgery, like his house on the river, is built with traditional materials, slate, harling and Scottish rounded shapes, but in an unusual, highly modern way creating a very relaxed and interesting interaction of building and landscape, pleasant to encounter.

The Medical Centre

At the end of Inch Road the 1960s fire station employs modern materials–steel, concrete and plate glass–in a very direct and expressive way and its tower, 'decorated' by its balconies, gives it the feeling of civic intention while the red doors convey something of the excitment of the fire brigade. Seen against the backdrop of the trees of the Broomlands estate it makes a satisfactory end piece to Edensie Road and is a meaningful landmark in the town.

It makes a suitable place, too, to end this look at Kelso, where I think the layering of time was very well displayed, the changes not only in the pattern of the town but in the re-ordering of Floors Castle and the parish church over the years as circumstances changed. This showed up in the place names, and with the other serendipities: the Pilkington Church, Ednam House and Rennie's Bridge, left an unforgettable image of 'place' imprinted on the memory.

Summary

WHAT DID WE LEARN?

In the introduction chapter it was suggested that the buildings of the burghs would have two tales to tell: the story of the burghs' history or development, and the buildings' story, the story of architecture. This turned out largely to be the case ,but everywhere we visited there seemed to be another fascinating tale about people, not ordinary people but extraordinary people who did things or caused them to happen. What was unexpected, in view of the small size and widespread geographic distribution of the burghs, was how proliflic the extraordinary was, in people, in buildings.

PLACE

In looking round these six very different Scottish burghs certain common factors readily emerged. All of them were originally associated with a castle, all were planted towns, even though there may have been a previous settlement and all were sited in strong defensible positions, adjacent to a river, often navigable, and astride a road. The river was essential, a source of water for drinking, for sanitation, for industrial processing–mills, tanneries, bleachfields etc.– even of fish for food. All had had in their time not only a church but houses of the monastic orders and some a cathedral or an abbey, in which case the burgh was usually erected in favour of the Bishop or Abbot.

   Clearly the castle, the church and burgh were integrally linked and it was no surprise to discover that the siting and structure of the burghs was part of a politcal programme, the enfeudalisation of Scotland, a programme aimed at national control and development. King David I was architect of this programme and four of our six burghs were planted in, or by, his time.

   An interesting paradox was the contrast between their local role, as closed, inward-looking, monopolistic societies, and their national role with links to the King, and later to Parliment, and through the merchants, monasteries and church, to England and Europe, two widely differing cultural influences.

   Dumfries's Bridge and Stirling's Castle and walls aside, little now remained of the medieval save ruins–Scotland's violent early history assured that. Nevertheless, in every burgh the original planted form still showed as a footprint on the ground, mapping the old narrow rigs, the markets and even the location of the walls.

   The characteristic stone vernacular buildings of the burghs were seen to date from the sixteenth-century onward, after the Reformation, when more settled times and the secularisation of the monasteries provided the opportunities, the land and the found-materials for building on a wider scale.

Following the Act of Union, and despite a growing loss of monopoly power a new era of burghal prosperity was clearly ushered in, brought about by improvements in agriculture and wider access to markets formerly closed to Scottish merchants. The growth of wealth and with it a 'gentle' society, led to a wave of fashionable building within the burghs. Old institutions were rebuilt in the image of the new times, and the towns became the focus of social life for the surrounding areas, as travel on the new roads became safer and easier. This was when the stately tolbooths, grand parish churches, dignified hospitals, high schools and academies were built, and alms houses, and town houses with front gardens all began to appear. Inns, assembly rooms, masonic halls and museums followed as the burghs became parts of the total urban culture of the nation, and tourism essentially began. The Enlightenment flourished and so did Dissension, and churches proliferated as congregations divided and divided again.

Steam and the industrial revolution completed the process: the railways brought commuters, settlers, whose wealth earned elsewhere was spent on enhancing and enlarging the burghs. They built grand new villas and houses, and new wide modern roads insettlements beyond the walls, which, with their gates, were often removed at this time. A growing municipal pride built new town and public halls, libraries, and drill halls, prisons, factories and all the trimmings of an expanding industrial culture followed, including cholera brought by piped water and sewage plants. In the present century the freedom of movement of goods and people conferred by the internal combustion engine could be seen to have brought about even more rapid change, a spreading out of the towns accompanied by massive re-construction in the centre, a process now belatedly being checked as the conservation and 'green' movements make us all environmentally aware, and increasing Europeanisation and tourism make us conscious of our heritage, and our differences as well as our similarities.

All this, from the medieval ruins to the ubiquitous chain stores and devastating parking lots, was there to be seen in some degree or another in every burgh we visited, a reading if you will, of how the burgh had grown.

BUILDINGS

Each burgh also had architectural gems and surprises of its own.

Stirling had its castle, grander really than Edinburgh's, more medieval, redolent with atmosphere, but it also had a wonderful and unexpected Victorian rogue architect who built perhaps the earliest steel-framed building in Britain, with its own electricity generator too, a building eccentric and eclectic in its bold forms, as was his other, *'art Nouveau'* block in Friar's Wynd with its curious mottoes. In Stirling, too, the Victorian 'new town' outside the walls was particularly clear, while in Dumfries the medieval and the Georgian architectural contribution were still extant to a surprising degree. But who would have expected to find Britain's first concrete-framed factory built by a famous American architect, Albert Khan, in this quiet country town. A powerful functionalist building, it is matched by the earlier but equally functional working Georgian corn-mill in the village of New Abbey, nearby.

Kelso was ducal and grand, a ruined Norman abbey, two magnified classical offerings in Ednam House with its wonderful ceilings, and Floors Castle with its grand apartments, and estate; but again there was the unexpected, the excitement of Pilkington's rogue Victorian church with its curious hidden entrance and grotesque tower, and Rennie's grand classic bridge; the quieter charm too of the contemporary fire station and health centre, not to mention the art deco high school.

The old and new towns side by side, and the splendid Homeric atomic power station were Thurso's treat and elegant Elgin was a classical *tour de force*, its high street stretching from the castle to the cathedral, with a Janus-like church in the middle and the classic domed and lanterned hospital and institution presiding over each entrance to the town. But, once again, did we expect the Edwardian rogue terrace and bungalow, with their looted 'Spynie Palace' details, or the little classic 'Scottish thirties' bungalow in Wittet Drive and a working water-mill and Basil Spence town hall thrown in. Elgin was where the power of patronage and its contribution to architecture could be most clearly seen.

Paisley, perhaps, was the biggest surprise of all, the modern tenement town which turned out to be historical, with its splendid newly found medieval drain (or secret passage), its mostly 'fake' medieval abbey and the biggest, most lavish Baptist church in Europe. On top of that it had vast Victorian mills and awesome ruins and the finest collection of public monuments on a skyline anywhere outside Edinburgh. There too we found the work of two fascinating home-grown architects: McLennan, an engineer architect, bizarrely exploring '*art noveau*', and Tait, the finest Scottish architect of his generation and co-ordinator of the Great Empire Exhibition, demonstrating the main stream modern at its best. Plus a town-full of fascinating tenements, removing any thought that this building type need ever be monotonous.

The architectural heritage of these six burghs proved rich and multi-faceted, and for me, an inspiration to delve further, to follow up on the architects and buildings we discovered. I hope others will be similarly excited and interested by what there is to be seen, if you make an effort to look.

For me too, there was the presence of order, in the planned towns, in the great buildings like the cathedrals, abbeys and palaces, as well as, in different ways, in the mill complex in Paisley, or the great house of Floors. But there was the pleasure of disorder too, to be found in the backlands of Elgin and Kelso behind the street façades, or in the huddled fishing town of Thurso. And everywhere the layering of time, the alterations and overlays the centuries brought to Stirling Castle, Kelso Parish Church, Elgin's High Street, Dumfries town centre, or Kelso's Square.

What a rich architectural scene to be found in a small country with so few building materials and such limited wealth.

PEOPLE

Surprises were not confined to buildings or places, however; we scarcely visited a single town without learning about special people who had lived, or visited, or even left there. Wallace, Bruce and Mary Queen of Scots, even Burns scratching his window in Stirling, perhaps were to be expected; but Frank Branwell, the designer of the Blenheim and Beaufort bombers, or Dummond the great tractarian—did we expect to find them in Stirling? And again, did Dumfries not only have Bruce and Wallace, and Burns again, but Burns in a paddle-steamer; and Barrie and Peter Pan too, not to mention two great inventive bankers, Paterson with his Bank of England and Bank of Scotland, and the Revd Henry Duncan and the Trustee Savings Bank.

We found Walter Scott at school in Kelso, and an unknown pastry cook who modelled a castle in matchsticks and icing sugar, as well as John Knox's nephew, and a Duke with two family trees. Burns and Bonnie Prince Charlie were both visitors there, while in the remote north, Thurso was revealed as the home not only the founder if the Boys' Brigade, Sir William Smith, but also the instigator of the Statistical Accounts of Scotland, Sir John Sinclair, town planner extraordinary; and John Gow, the Orkney Pirate.

Edward I, the 'Hammer of the Scots' had stayed twice in Elgin, and Macbeth died there, while two great nabobs who had made their fortunes in faraway India returned to embellish wonderfully their remote little town, confirmation surely of the need to belong, to identify with somewhere, or some community? Dickson similarly made his fortune in Havana and London yet returned to Kelso to belong again in the later years of his life.

Something, perhaps, most clearly seen in Paisley, was that communities have a character of their own, a mixture of their history, their occupations or preoccupations, and perhaps the 'genius loci', the place itself. The Revd. Witherspoon of American Declaration of Independence fame and William Wallace, patriot, are both Paisley people; so was Tannahill, the rebellious poet, and Stowe, the educationalist and the great Paisley entrepreneurs, the Coats, the Cochranes and the Galbraiths; all out of one burgh, one small town, but a town which as it grew invited Pavlova and Kean and Charlie Chaplin all to play, and Harriet Beecher Stowe to present Uncle Tom's Cabin.

Thus the very real pleasure of the architectural discoveries was matched by the discovery of fascinating people and the realisation of how the Scottish nation was shaped by its people as well as its kings, and that the royal strategy of the planned burghs as instruments of civilisation had worked, and the story of that civilisation was there, tangible in every burgh we visited.

GLOSSARY

Domestic

Abutment	Solid masonry placed to resist and balance the sideways thrust of an arch or vault.
Advice Stane	A carved lintel to door or window
Causey	Stones set in the centre of the street, raised clear of the gutters and reserved for the richer citizens
Clubskew	The end stone at the base of a gable, also called a skewput. Often enriched by carving
Crowstep or corbiestep	(Corbie is the old Scots word for crow). Stone 'steps' on gable, which could be used for access to ridge, or, with planks from gable to gable, to repair any part of the roof.
Elevations	The vertical faces of a building
Enrichment	The ornament used in the decorative elaboration of a member of a building
Freestone	Stone which can easily be worked either way, therefore ideal for carving
Gable	The triangular upper part of a wall at the end of a roof with sloping sides
Hallan Stane	The threshold stone at the door
Harling	Roughcast applied to walls to protect the stonework
Hipped roof	Having sloping end instead of vertical gables
Keystone	The central topmost stone of an arch
Lantern	Part of an upper structure such as a tower, pierced with windows and open below to the main body of a building
Loft	A gallery
Lossan Nail	Diamond-shape headed nail, with which plank doors were studded before the introduction of pannelled doors in the 17th century
Marriage lintel	Advice stone with two sets of initials and date

Pantile	Clay tiles, possibly originally imported from Holland. (From Finnish 'paan'—a shingle)
Parapet	A low wall at the edge of a roof
Pier	A support of masonry designed to sustain vertical pressure; a pillar from which an arch springs.
Pigg	Chimney pot (1577 house)
Port	A gate or gateway; a gatehouse
Precinct	The ground immediately surrounding a religious house or cathedral, usually marked out by a boundary wall
Reveals	Stonework surrounding doors and windows
Roughcast	Sandlime plaster cast with small stones used to cover walls
Sash and case window	Comprises two glazed wooden frames (the sash) which may be divided by astragals into several panes each, each sash sliding within a frame (the case) counterbalanced by ropes and weights
Setts	Rectangular whinstone blocks used as road surface
Sill	The lower horizontal part of a window frame
String course	A narrow horizontal line of projecting masonry carried along a building
Thackstane	A projecting, sloping stone at a chimney to throw water onto thatch
Turnpike Stair	An external spiral staircase
Vault	An arched roof or ceiling of stone
Vestibule	An antechamber or lobby

Ecclesiastical

Aisle	(in the context of Elgin) part of a church parallel to, and divided by arcades from, the nave, choir or presbytery
Arcade	A range of arches carried on pillars
Ashlar	Stone accurately cut or squared to given dimensions; thin facing of squared stones to cover brick or rubble walls

Aumbry	A cupboard or wall-recess
Bas-relief	A sculpture in low relief
Belfry	The storey of a tower in which the bells are hung
Boss	An ornamental knob or projection at the intersection of ribs in a vault
Buttress	Masonry built against or projecting from a wall to give additional strength; or ornamental masonry imitating such a structural device
Canon	A member of the chapter, i.e. the body of ecclesiastics associated with a cathedral or religious house
Canopy	A roof-like projection extending over a door, window, tomb, niche, etc.
Chanonry	(Scots) the area containing the dwellings of the cathedral dignitaries and office-bearers
Chapter-house	The place of assembly for the dean, office-bearers and canons of a cathedral, or the equivalent dignitaries of a monastery, to discuss business
Choir	The area of the church containing the stalls (i.e. seats) of the clergy and choristers who performed the daily round of services.
Choir-stalls	Wooden seats in the choir, often elaborately carved and provided with wooden canopies.
Clerestory	The antique spelling of the word disguises its meaning of a 'clear storey'
Consecration Cross	A cross usually enclosed within a circle, carved on the walls of a church to mark the dedication of the building to its sacred purpose.
Corbel	A projecting stone block supporting a member above
Crocket	A decoration in gothic architecture carved in leaf shapes, regularly spaced on spires, pinnacles, gables, canopies, etc.
Crossing	The intersection of the main body of a church with its transepts
Cusps	Small projecting points in gothic tracery
Finial	A formalised flower ornament at the top of a pinnacle, canopy, etc.
Lancet	A high narrow opening terminating in a pointer arch

Manse	An ecclesiastical residence
Mouldings	The contours or shapes carved in members of a building
Nave	The part of a church open to the laity
Niche	A recess or hollow in a wall, usually to contain a statue
Ogee	An arch composed of double-curved or S-shaped arcs
Piscina	A stone for washing the vessel of Holy Communion
Portal	A doorway
Prelate	An ecclesiastical dignitary of high rank especially a bishop
Quatrefoil	An opening or decorative detail having its outline so divided by curvilinear projecting points as to give it the appearance of four leaves or petals
Respond	A half-pillar bonded into a wall and carrying one end of an arch
Retable	A frame enclosing decorated panels above the back of an altar
Rood screen	A screen across the east end of the nave, on which was raised a painted representation of the Crucifixtion (the Anglo-Saxon word 'rood' meaning cross)
Sacristy	Repository for vestments, etc. in a church
Sedilia	Stone seats for clergy recessed into the south wall of the presbytery or the chancel
Spire	A tall structure rising from a tower and terminating in a point
Stall	A carved seat of wood or stone, usually in a row of similar seats
Tracery	The decorative work in the upper part of a window or panel
Transept	The arms at right angles to the main body of a cross-shaped church
Trefoil	An opening or decorative detail having its outline so divided by curvilinear projecting points as to give it the appearance of a three-lobed leaf
Triforium	The gallery or arcade in the wall over the arches at the sides of the main body of a large church, being at the level of the aisle roofs
Vesica	An upright almond shape